How to Preach More Powerful Sermons

How to Preach
More Powerful Sermons
Homer K. Buerlein

The Westminster Press
Philadelphia

Scripture quotations from the Revised Standard Version of the Bible are copyrighted 1946, 1952, © 1971, 1973 by the Division of Christian Education of the National Council of the Churches of Christ in the U.S.A. and are used by permission.

Book design by Gene Harris

Published by The Westminster Press®
Philadelphia, Pennsylvania

PRINTED IN THE UNITED STATES OF AMERICA

9 8 7 6 5 4 3 2 1

Library of Congress Cataloging-in-Publication Data

Buerlein, Homer K., 1920–
    How to preach more powerful sermons.

    1. Preaching.   I. Title.
BV4211.2.B825   1986   251   85–26378
ISBN 0–664–24683–4 (pbk.)

Contents

Foreword

Here is a book that can be read with profit by ministers or seminarians—by anyone who has the awesome responsibility of ascending the pulpit stairs to preach.

Most books on preaching are written by preachers or teachers of preachers. The voices of those in the congregation are seldom heard. I cannot recall a book on preaching by a consumer of the preacher's wares. My friend H. K. Buerlein has finally given us one.

Connoisseurs of the arts often write about the arts, and artists listen. Mr. Buerlein is, in his own way, a connoisseur of preaching, and preachers would do well to listen.

Mr. Buerlein makes no pretense at expertise in biblical criticism, exegesis, or hermeneutics. His concern is not with the depths of sermon content but with the exterior dress in which the sermon appears: how it is titled, how it is begun, how it is structured, how it is delivered, how it ends.

If you are turned off by such "surface" matters, let me remind you that the listener encounters the surface first of all. If the exterior dress of the sermon is unattractive, if the surface is dull and opaque, the person in the pew will never get to the depths, no matter how deep they may be. Scientists may spend a lifetime trying to discover what is inside the proverbial black box. Sermon listeners do not have that much patience or curiosity.

One thing I can promise you. Whether you agree or disagree with the writer, you will find this book easy to read. The author reaches out and engages you in conversation. He is forthright and unabashed in presenting his point of view. I found the book difficult to put down.

Albert Curry Winn

Prologue

"How dare you, a layman, try to tell me how to preach!"

You have every right to say that. Although I am a professional speaker, a speechwriter, and a teacher of public speaking, does that qualify me to write a book about preaching?

Well, I've been going to church for fifty-five years—and have heard a lot of preaching. For the last thirty years, I have tried to be a responsible Presbyterian layman. I have also had a unique vantage point. As chairman for many years of a business luncheon group founded partly for the purpose of hearing the views of clergy of all faiths, I not only introduced many preachers, priests, and rabbis, I also enjoyed them as table companions and got to know many of them personally and professionally.

This long association with the clergy of many churches was paralleled by my own frequent public speaking engagements, as well as by occasional stints of teaching this art to others. As I criticized messages by business leaders, it seemed virtually impossible to keep from evaluating sermons in the same light.

But, you ask, "Why this book?" I wrote it because I felt I had something to contribute to the kingdom as a result of this experience, both in teaching and in public speaking, and because of a nagging propensity for critiquing sermons.

This book makes no claims to theological depth, my knowledge of that subject being limited to what I learned teaching Sunday school—mostly to lively adults—over the years. Our concern here is rather with the task of making biblical preaching a matter of vital interest to the person in the pew.

I'm encouraged by the observations of others in pinpointing the enormous value of the sermon in the life of a church. As Kevin H. Axe, a Catholic lay author, wrote, "It's almost impossible to overemphasize the importance of the sermon in the minds of the laity. A bad sermon is much worse than a waste of time; repeatedly bad sermons can seriously wound and finally kill the spirit of the assembled community." Or, as the insightful Dr. John H. Leith, Pemberton Professor of Theology at Union Theological Seminary in Virginia, put it in his book *An Introduction to the Reformed Tradition,* "The Christian community forfeits its own greatest opportunity when it minimizes the significance of preaching. The effectiveness of preaching is difficult to measure. Yet it is a documentable fact that over a period of years the quality of preaching determines in significant measure the quality of a congregation's life."

I've always been a copious note taker and will leave practically every spiritual address with a pocketful of notes. (You'll find here firm encouragements to do the same.) After years of observations and notes, I feel I have come to understand the sermon as have few other lay people, and I'm absolutely convinced of the need for sound techniques in bringing the congregation to an awareness that God is present in the house of worship. These techniques are the grist of this book.

It would mean a great deal to me if my efforts, through this book, might in some way start a repayment of the great debt I owe ministers for their spiritual support and guidance throughout my life. I shall be most grateful if this volume, then, helps them to better proclaim the Word of God and the salvation of Jesus Christ.

                                                           H.K.B.

Acknowledgments

My thanks to:

Dr. William J. Carl III, formerly Professor of Homiletics at Union Theological Seminary of Virginia, now the minister of First Presbyterian Church, Dallas, Texas, for his suggestions and encouragement.

Dr. Albert Curry Winn, former Moderator of the Presbyterian Church U.S., past president of Louisville Presbyterian Seminary and my earlier minister for nine years, currently minister of the North Decatur Presbyterian Church, Decatur, Georgia, who is a master preacher without peer in the use of two sermon arts highlighted in this writing, the pause and the conclusion, for his consistently outstanding sermons, which epitomize the high-quality pulpit presence toward which this book is directed.

Dr. Jerry Tarver, Professor of Speech Communications, University of Richmond, and a giant in that field, for his enthusiastic reception of the concept of this project and for valuable suggestions that came out of his vast teaching experience in the area of public speaking.

Dr. W. Landon Miller, retired minister of the Northminster Baptist Church of Richmond, Virginia, who advised me on a number of theological blank spots and whose superb extemporaneous preaching contributed to my now firm belief in the strength of that style.

Dora, my wife, for her encouragement and invaluable editorial and proofreading assistance.

Bob, my elder son, who nagged me constantly to hurry up and complete this book on the basis that I would not have a valid excuse for St. Peter, who would one day severely chastise me if I did not finish it in my lifetime.

And for permission to reprint and quote from these publications and persons:

Dr. Fred B. Speakman, retired minister of Third Presbyterian Church, Pittsburgh, Pennsylvania, for excerpts from an address.

Dr. John H. Leith, Pemberton Professor of Theology, Union Theological Seminary in Virginia, for an excerpt from his book *An Introduction to the Reformed Tradition* (John Knox Press).

Dr. Joseph Lee Vaughan, former Professor of English, University of Virginia, for excerpts from his book *Oral Communications.*

McGraw-Hill Book Company, for excerpts from William G. Hoffman's *Public Speaking for Business Men.*

Macmillan Publishing Company, for excerpts from Robert W. Kirkpatrick's *The Creative Delivery of Sermons.*

Tribune Media Services, for an excerpt from "A Talented, Hard-Working Professional Actor" by Andy Rooney.

The Westminster Press, for an excerpt from Robert D. Young's *Be Brief About It.*

The Wall Street Journal, for excerpts from an article.

Trial Magazine (Association of Trial Lawyers of America), for excerpts from "Friendly Persuasion" (August 1981).

1

Strengthening the Delivery
of the Sermon

Many a sermon is given a magnificent aura by the infectious nature of the preacher and a skillful delivery. But what bother me are those dutifully researched and composed sermons that are totally devoid of a pleasingly persuasive and appealing presentation. This is one of the reasons why I've tackled this book. This first chapter, then, will address what might be called pulpit behavior. It will involve how the sermon is "served."

This subject is well addressed in the foreword to Robert Kirkpatrick's *The Creative Delivery of Sermons:* "Teachers of homiletics have correctly assumed that the content of a sermon can have no adequate substitute in the voice and manner of its delivery. But the vehicle of expression is as important to a sermon as transports are to troops in war. The power of a sermon is measured at the point of contact with the pew."

Why Is Style So Important?

During World War II, and several months after the D-Day invasion, I was stationed in France. I got a couple of days' leave and stopped at a small restaurant in a nearby town. France, as you know, was pretty well ravaged when the Germans retreated. There was little food available. The only things on the menu were soup, bread and cheese, and a limited supply of white wine. The fare was skimpy, not much to behold. But the service—oh, that service!—made me feel like a king. The waiter produced the soup—which was rather thin—with a flourish that would cause admiration on the part of New York's best restaurateurs. The bread and cheese were served as if they were pheasant under glass. The food was nothing by normal standards, but the way it was served turned the whole meal into a memorable experience.

If "served" properly, a sermon also can be a memorable experience. This is not to suggest for one moment that if you develop your style you can ease off on the research and time-consuming preparation of the sermon's content. No way! But if you can prepare a substantive, persuasive, meaningful, soul-searching—even a soul-saving—message and *then* deliver it in the style it deserves, your mastery of this area of your ministry is assured.

Dr. Fred B. Speakman, the renowned minister of Third Presbyterian Church in Pittsburgh, now retired, once participated in a panel on homiletics at an annual Bible conference at Massanetta Springs, Virginia. The subject under discussion was the style of various preachers. He said about Dr. James S. Stewart, the Scottish Presbyterian pastor who was chaplain to the Queen, "James Stewart is the dullest cat at a party you ever saw in your life. But when he steps into the pulpit, the moment he opens his mouth, that congregation—well, it's as if you plugged them all in on his frequency. I swear James Stewart could read the telephone directory and people would sit there entranced."

This is the style all preachers should try to master.

Words Written vs. Words Spoken

I once visited a church in which the minister delivered what seemed at the time to be an interesting sermon, but I couldn't quite grasp the real thrust of the message, because it was delivered in a monotone, most of it read with little warmth or enthusiasm. After the service, I bumped into a delightful woman, I think she was the church secretary, who recognized me as a stranger and greeted me.

She pointed out that her minister always made copies of his sermons available in mimeographed form. At my request, she agreed to mail me a copy of the sermon I'd just heard.

When the sermon arrived in the mail and I read it, I realized that the structure of the message was coherent and sound and the points well made. I could hardly believe I was reading the same sermon I'd heard.

In the quietness of my den, I began reading the sermon aloud, with feeling, emphasis, and enthusiasm. It occurred to me again that this was potentially a powerful sermon, and I started over, this time trying it on my tape recorder. You'd be surprised what a fine sermon it was, played back. I added some slight body movements and gestures (see chapter 13) and ended up with a much better presentation.

The Lasting Impressions of Style

Back in 1979, Yale University president Bartlett Giamatti commented on then-president Jimmy Carter's oratory: "The junctures don't receive the inflection, the punch. In a sense, style is substance, and with Carter, there's a gap that widens there. There's a theatrical dimension that's absent. Carter's speech is out of synch. As if it were dubbed."

That same year, a Hollywood reporter who reviewed the Academy Awards presentations admitted to being touched by the gentleness and beauty of Sir Laurence Olivier's acceptance speech for a special award. The reporter went on to say that upon rereading the speech, it turned out to have little or no meaning. The effect of the words was all in the feeling and the style of Olivier's delivery. Sometimes, it's not so much *what* is said but *how*.

For many years I served as chairman of the business luncheon held every Friday at our church. Aside from frequent presiding duties, I had to coordinate the speakers' roster with the other six members of the committee. Our format for speakers alternated between lay people and ministers.

This committee would often invite back for a second, third, or even fourth time a speaker we knew would do a good job. This obviated the gamble of ending up with a poor speaker or, as they were sometimes uncharitably referred to, a clunker. Now this is the interesting point: Often a committee member would say something like "Yes, let's have the Rev. John Jones again. The last time he was here he gave a wonderful talk." In many such cases, I would prod the committee member making this suggestion with the question, "That's fine, but what did he talk about?" Almost invariably, the committee person would say, "I can't remember exactly what he said, but I do remember that it was a terrific talk."

I'm sure you've done exactly what I've done regarding preachers or speakers you've heard. Just mention the name of a preacher, and I have an instant recollection of the quality of his preaching. Like the committee member just mentioned, I can grade that person from A to F insofar as pulpit presentations are concerned, but I would be hard pressed to recall many of the sermons in detail. We all may remember flashes of brilliance, but to be asked to sit down and write out the themes of more than half a dozen of any great preacher's sermons would be an arduous proposition for most of us. But we'll never forget the *style* of these preachers.

Confirming the psychology of the rememberability of style vs. content is this quote from the August 1981 issue of *Trial,* the monthly publication of the Association of Trial Lawyers of America. An article entitled "Friendly Persuasion" states:

> Impressions, not content, decide cases. Jurors have difficulty in the courtroom because of their unfamiliarity with trial procedure and their inability to absorb everything that occurs in the court-room.
>
> Jurors are interrogated by lawyers. They receive conflicting testimony from witnesses. They receive arguments from lawyers. They receive instructions from the judge. In the jury room, each of them is an originator and receiver of communication. As a result, most of the content is lost in this process, and what remains is essentially an impression. *It is the impression, based upon presentation, rather than the content of the presentation itself that is most important to persuasion* [emphasis added].

Winston Churchill is a good person to study from the standpoint of content and delivery. He had a lot to say, and he said it in a deliberate, forceful, and commanding manner. His voice had the ring of authority. But did you know that in his earlier days he was a terrible speaker? He had a weak voice, stuttered, and even had a lisp. Believe it or not, he actually fainted just before he was scheduled to speak in the House of Commons. He overcame what appeared to be insurmountable odds in this area by first mastering the art of writing his speeches. Then, after he labored over every word he was going to say, he trained himself to utter convincingly every single one of those words. He was first a writer and then a speaker. But once he learned the proper savoring and emphasizing of words, he became as much a speaker as a writer. If you are ever in a position to hear recordings of his speeches, you will note that each word seems like a precious jewel worthy of individual attention.

In a 1982 *Wall Street Journal* review of a Broadway play that starred Jessica Tandy and Hume Cronyn, the drama critic said, "The Cronyns know that great acting—like life itself—is built of little pieces." In the same way, good sermons are made of little pieces: different bits of voice inflections, pauses, varying emphases—anything but a one-paragraph drone.

A 1977 news article relates the implication of theatrical acting to proper sermon style. It describes a workshop requested by sixteen Methodist clergy. The star panelist was a voice and movement director for a theater in the Midwest. She said to this class of preachers, "Ministers as a group are pretty dull in the pulpit. I remember as a child that the only time they had any passion was when they were telling me I would die and go to hell. They should use that passion to get me as interested in living and helping and doing for others." She went on to say that ministers normally talk *at* her, instead of sharing what they know *with* her. At the end of the session, one minister said, "We were taught to write sermons but never before to really preach them."

In summary, remember that the manner of the preacher and the content of the sermon reach the congregation at almost the same time. This situation demands that the preacher make a good impression through style as well as through solid, well-organized sermon material. Failure in *either* area will be noticeable and diminishes the effectiveness of the sermon. Always keep in mind, too, that the congregation will remember the image of the preacher presenting the sermon much longer than exactly what the preacher said. The manner and tone of the preacher are critically important. The congregation, unfortunately, will recall sermons primarily in terms of their total impact rather than in content details.

Selecting Your Style

Even if you've not been trained in various methods of speaking, common sense will indicate that you have only three choices. You can use notes in a manuscript style, you can use partial—or prompting—notes to guide you, or you can use no notes at all.

Manuscript

Without a doubt, the reading of a manuscript is the safest way to deliver a sermon. You've spent a lot of time translating your conclusions into words, and you simply read them one by one, without missing a beat. This method, however, presents the problem of trying to get a good conversational tone into the sermon. Besides losing the opportunity for proper inflections, one's physical motion (see chapter 13) is limited. In short, you are left only with words.

In reading, the preacher cannot make good eye contact with the congregation. Anyone at all skillful with this style may recognize the need to look up from the paper occasionally. But even then, it is difficult to become at all close to the congregation. As I heard one congregant say after hearing such a sermon read, "If the preacher's going to read it, it's better to give me a copy and save us both time."

There are times when, for the sake of absolute understanding and clarity, certain phrases should be read. But this is the exception. In some areas, this method is more readily accepted. For instance, the President of the United States may have to read his message to the nation and to Congress because the occasions are unusually formal and dignified and call for precision, conciseness, and accuracy.

Without a doubt, the deadliest combination of inadequacies in a sermon is the construction of a one-point, one-paragraph sermon that is read—and read poorly. Yet this is the fare to which many congregations are subjected and which many preachers feel should be accepted.

I beg of you, study and pray for the power to break the umbilical cord between you and the word-by-word manuscript type of presentation.

Memorized

The opposite form of presentation, requiring the use of no notes at all, is that of preaching from a memorized manuscript. You're really asking for trouble on this one. You'll need both an elephantine memory and nerves of steel. I used this method all the time until, on one fateful occasion, it struck back, and I'll never try it again.

The situation involved my having to introduce before a hundred or so assembled businessmen a well-known Methodist clergyman, Dr. A. Purnell Bailey, whom I had introduced at least half a dozen times before and who was a personal friend. When I got to "It gives me great pleasure and, indeed, a sense of honor to present to you again our speaker of the day—" I forgot his name! I stood there before these dozens of faces looking up expectantly for the announcement and sensing, I feared, my dilemma. I said what was perhaps my quickest prayer ever, to the effect that, if God would only allow me to remember this man's name, never again would I stand up in front of any group without some form of notes—containing, particularly, the name of the person to be introduced. Then I cleared my throat, feigning a slight cough, and somehow treaded water for about five seconds—which seemed more like five years—before the name miraculously appeared in my mind.

This happened to me after twenty years of doing this sort of thing. But it will never happen to me again.

You may feel your presentation will be smoother and more coherent with this method. But it's sometimes better not to be so smooth and to have a few hesitations and restatements than to be exposed to some of the potential pitfalls of a memorized sermon. Your concentration may tend to be on what word comes next, rather than to be centered on the congregation. A memorized sermon can also cause the preacher to develop a vague stare, because direct eye contact is harder to maintain. You are less concerned with communicating the message than with remembering and expressing the words. A memorized sermon, therefore, may come across to congregants more as a performance than any other of the methods available. Remember, a good sermon must be felt by the preacher and must be a part of the preacher. This feeling of sincerity about the topic will be weakened by the concentration required to remember the words.

Many people attempt to use this method. Such preachers look as if they're reading from an invisible screen mounted at the rear of the sanctuary. This style, in fact, is almost dangerously close to that of reading from a manuscript. And remember that memorizing a sermon requires that you spend a great deal of time, much of which the average minister does not have, memorizing the "lines."

Finally, the language of a memorized sermon has to be rather formal. It smacks of the essay and lacks the conversational intimacy you find in the extemporaneous sermon.

So unless you are unique in the area of sermonizing, you had better avoid this second method also.

Extemporaneous

Now we come to the method of presentation that is the easiest and yet by far the most effective type of presentation: the extemporaneous sermon.

From the standpoint of semantics, there should be one clarification. The word "extemporaneous" is often defined as: composed, performed, or uttered on the spur of the moment. A second meaning is: carefully prepared but delivered without notes or text. In using this word, I mean neither of these definitions but, rather, the extemporaneous speaking from prepared notes. In other words, this section has to do with preaching *after preparation* rather than simply off the cuff—as the word "extemporaneous" seems to imply.

This preparation requires the composition of a series of skeletal notes that keep you right on top of the sermon body, point by point. It allows you the freedom to extemporize from these points in a fresh, intimate, and conversational manner.

The greatest sermon format you can possibly come up with is one that allows you freedom of thought during your delivery —a freedom that permits you to choose or reject words as you go. This requires a familiarity with the subject to the point that you'll simply be carrying on a conversation about it with the congregation, guided by your notes, which will keep you from wandering off the subject or getting lost.

This method is particularly beneficial as it relates to the practicing of your sermon (see chapter 16). It also allows you enough space on the page to place all sorts of cues regarding voice inflections and pulpit movements (see chapter 13).

To repeat what was said about manuscript reading, there may be certain thoughts you'll want to write out for accuracy's sake, to be read in the midst of your extemporizing. It may be difficult to switch gears into this spot of reading word-by-word without violating the more natural tone and inflections of the extemporaneous speaking that has come first. One minister in using this approach actually said to his congregation, "To make sure that both you and I do not misunderstand the content and importance of this conclusion, I want to read it slowly, word by word." And his tone and delivery style *did* change, but at least the congregation was prepared for it, and nobody dropped a stitch.

Dr. Norman Vincent Peale preaches without notes and without being behind the pulpit. If he wishes to quote a letter or something else lengthy, he will pull it out of his robe and read it.

Here's another example of the force behind extemporaneous preaching. A preacher friend who felt close enough to ask my opinion about certain areas of his preaching once said, "It looks like my Sunday attendance is falling off, and I'm getting fewer compliments about my sermons. Do you have any feelings about this?" Having known this fellow for some time, I knew he wanted an honest response, so I gave him one. I reminded him that he read practically all of his sermons, and although he read them skillfully, it created the impression that he was preaching "at" the congregation rather than "to" them. This meant that he was taking his sermons word by word from the pages in front of him and laying them out word by word in front of his congregation. But if he would only pass on, extemporaneously, his usually very good sermon points idea by idea, he would be persuading his congregation—he would be conversing with his congregation—he would be talking to them rather than at them.

2

The Challenge of Finding Effective Titles

There are any number of works on the art of preaching. In the process of reading them, I've found myself taking friendly issue with some of the positions put forth by various authors on some aspects of that skill.

Take the choice of a sermon title, for instance. This is a most important exercise. I was dismayed to read in some books on homiletics that titling a sermon isn't really important. One book maintained that a good title helps create interest in the subject, but no great effort should be expended in trying to come up with a catchy one. Really? Let me tell you why you should place a *great deal* of importance on sermon titling.

From my side of the pulpit, there seems to be a good-sized group of people who move from Sunday to Sunday among various churches. They are persons who never quite seem to find the ideal congregation and apparently prefer to become "floaters." Often they will eventually become members of the church where the personal attractiveness of the preacher or the sociability of the congregation pleases them.

Several of these floaters have confided that they consult the Saturday afternoon newspaper to check the sermon titles for Sunday services. This method of operation is also followed by faithful members of a given church who, not finding in their own minister's Sunday-to-Sunday preaching everything they had hoped for, wander a bit from the fold. Occasionally a friend will call me on a Saturday night to say that he is disenchanted with his pastor's upcoming message and is going down the street to a closer church simply because that minister's sermon has a provocative and intriguing title.

Weak Titles, Weak Reactions

While one purpose of good titling is to help the minister with the focus of the sermon, it also attracts more people into church. In the process, a soul or two may be saved. Imagine the typical college student on Easter morning facing the usual Sunday morning question: "Shall I go to church or sack in a little longer?"

Imagine this student crawling out of bed reluctantly, locating Saturday afternoon's paper and searching through the church page for the sermon titles at two nearby churches. "The Empty Tomb" is listed for the closer church. The student knows that the sermon will be equally predictable. After all, ministers have very little flexibility on Easter morning in that they must talk about the resurrection.

Next the student looks at the program listed at the other church, a few blocks farther down the street. Here the sermon topic is "The Stone Rolled Away." The student is probably thinking by now, So what else is new? This is not a criticism of either the minister or the topic. It's simply difficult to become interested enough to get dressed and make the trek to church.

Provocative Titles, Positive Reactions

What would the reaction and receptivity be to a title such as "Last Year's Easter Parade" or "Rabbits and Rabble-Rousers"? These titles aren't meant to be cute, but they are designed to provide some incentive for both churched and unchurched to want to attend simply because they deduce that a provocative title means a stirring sermon. Though I just invented these titles, let's continue with the sermons: "Last Year's Easter Parade"—the shallowness of millinery vs. the remembrance of the cross; "Rabbits and Rabble-Rousers"— the naiveté of people who give priority to rabbits, candy, and eggs and those who (you and me) constantly crucify Christ and demand his death by our lack of love.

The church section of a recent Saturday afternoon's newspaper listed the sermon topics in various Protestant churches. If you were the college student just mentioned, would you be moved to attend any of the churches primarily because of these topics?

Baptism and the Holy Spirit   The Joyful Christian
Dependency   The Glory of God
Model for Ministry   Pentecost Experience
Christ for the World

Not a single one of these titles, chosen at random, would inspire me to go hear the sermon. How about you? I might go out of loyalty to my church, or out of a desire to enjoy a sense of Christian fellowship, or (if I am musically inclined) to join in the singing and hear the renditions of the choir.

Now let me give you two sermon titles also listed on that page and see what you think of them. One was "In Defense of Beauty" and the other was "Somebody Is Calling My Name!"

For a moment, think of yourself as a lay person. Would you honestly feel pulled, tugged, moved, or otherwise enjoined— or anxious—to go to church in inclement weather to hear any of the sermons in the first group? How about the two sermons just listed? By the very freshness of their titles, it would seem that some real thought had been put into those sermons. My initial reaction would be that if the minister used the creativity required to come up with an unusual title, the sermon itself must be intriguing.

Ask yourself, does your title suggest that your sermon will be an event or a nonevent?

Series Building

A good sermon title can even spark ideas for a series of good topics. Take "bridge," for example. An initial sermon called "Building Bridges" could discuss Christian living. Comparisons could be made with the role of bridges in helping us get over obstacles and reaching our destinations. With the continuing problem of bridge maintenance being treated regularly in the press, it would be easy to discuss the need to properly plan and inspect a good "bridge."

Another sermon in this same series could discuss the need for Christian faith under the title "The Bridge Over the River Why," which might deal with suffering in the style of Job. Yet another could deal with Christianity in human conflict, as "A Bridge Over Troubled Waters," or with the impossibility of human perfection, as "A Bridge Too Far." Anyone who has ever watched all the episodes of a miniseries on TV knows the drawing power of a topic "to be continued"—though I'm certainly not suggesting we consider anything that remotely resembles a slick Broadway title.

When Title Scoops Message

There is one weak spot in the art of titling and topic selection: Too often the entire sermon is given away. Take the title "Practicing Christianity Through Love of God and Man." From that title, you know exactly what the preacher is going to say. You know, for instance, that a true Christian cannot love God without loving people, and vice versa. No doubt, numerous examples of each type of love will be present in the sermon.

Two newspaper clippings about lay speeches point up this same shortcoming. One article heralded an upcoming speech by a physician at a local academy of medicine, and his topic was "It's Your Academy—It's What You Make It!" What else is there to add to that title? You know exactly what he's going to say before he says it. Another such title was selected by a mechanical engineer addressing the convention dinner at an annual meeting of his peers: "The Interaction of Frictional Barriers Present in Lubrication Problems as Determined by Analytical Procedures." I'm no engineer, but isn't his entire talk contained in the title? In both cases, there is nothing intriguing or tempting about the titles. Little is left to the imagination.

To avoid declaring the whole message in the title, give it a twist to arouse curiosity. For instance, in the medical academy case speech, why not a title like "Blank Checks for M.D.s"? For the engineering group, how about "Homework on Lubrication Hazards"? (Though I'm still not sure I know what the subject is all about.)

How to Find Titles and Topics

There's no limit to the sources of potential sermon titles and topics. The few listed here are simply to make you more alert to these possibilities and get your mind working creatively in this area.

The Lectionary

From a lay person's standpoint there seem to be many advantages to the use of the ecumenical lectionary, if your church uses one, for sermon titles and topics.

- You're forced to look at passages in scripture otherwise overlooked.
- You must look at the entire Bible, rather than at sections.
- The lectionary provides maximum coherency throughout the year. You simply can't beat a good organizational plan, particularly when a series of related sermon topics is desired.
- Scripture is the lifeblood of the Christian community, and the whole of it should be discussed more frequently.
- The congregation is protected against their minister's favorite passages to the exclusion of other texts.
- It's difficult to accuse a minister of heresy in the area of topic-choosing if it comes from the lectionary (although what is done with that topic can be another matter).

To respect the lectionary, as pointed out by these advantages, is one thing; to be slavish in following it to the exclusion of topical flexibility is something altogether different.

Topical Themes

It's disappointing to see great events of national and international importance go unnoticed from the pulpit because they don't conform to the lectionary. Although they may not be appropriate as the complete sermon topic, such monumental events as man walking on the moon, the release of hostages from Iran or Lebanon, the election of a new President of the United States, and Voyager II making its headlong flight into the regions of Jupiter and Saturn are worth mention. It takes only slight flexibility and creativity to incorporate happenings such as these in a sermon. After all, they are important to listeners, and to include them indicates that the preacher shares their lives and interests. Also, lay people understand and react almost instantaneously to topical subjects.

If you find it difficult to include such events in your sermon, at least try to mention them in the morning pastoral prayer.

Where do topical sermon topics come from? And how can you make them sound like events rather than nonevents? Before getting into some of the sources of the sermon topics, consider this remarkable observation by Dr. Fred B. Speakman, then minister of Third Presbyterian Church in Pittsburgh:

"I pay a great deal of attention to so-called chance conversation. If you stay alert, you will hear people say the silliest and wisest things to their preacher about a number of things, and if you develop a third ear for listening, for even an absurd or wise comment from someone about life or themselves, you realize it is of interest and you've tapped something. That is one of the things I start carrying around in the back of my mind, wondering if it does not suggest a biblical framework. In time it will."

Let's go beyond Dr. Speakman's comment. One unusual way of selecting topics would be to take a survey. I've never seen a marketing/research study that didn't shock the sender. You'd be surprised, too, if you asked your congregation exactly what they wanted to hear by way of sermon topics. You might think they want to hear something about the missionary effort, nuclear proliferation, stewardship, or other subjects you'd like to preach about, but you could be amazed at their response. Don't discard the "receptive ear" approach.

The very thought of taking a survey may imply a lack of leadership and competence on the minister's part to compose sermon menus. You may feel strongly that ministers should give a congregation what they feel the congregation should get, rather than what they'd like to get.

The other side of the coin is that taking and using the survey can strengthen the pastor-congregation relationship when the congregation members realize that their wishes for sermon subjects are heeded. They may conclude that the minister is a person who wants to fill their sermonic needs as they subjectively feel them to be. If you prefer a less formal approach to such a survey—if, indeed, you are willing to attempt this kind of search for sermon topics at all—there's always the opportunity to introduce this subject during casual conversation with parishioners.

Apropos of giving some preference to the average churchgoer's wishes regarding topics, don't overlook such observances as George Washington's birthday, Mother's Day, Fourth of July, and Thanksgiving. This is not to turn a Sunday worship service into a Rotary Club meeting, but references to these occasions will strike for most members a sentimental chord that will make sermon reception stronger. And there are spiritual themes running through the character of these secular occasions.

One last word before getting into specifics. Try to have a wide variety of topics (the suggestions to come may be of help) so that your parishioners will think, These sermons are always interesting and inspiring; I wonder what my pastor will come up with next? That's one reason I'm opposed to the steady use of the lectionary and would prefer to see it alternated with a variety of other subjects.

The world is simply bulging with potential sermon titles and topics. They're all around us. One can't go through a single day without recognizing several possibilities. Listed here, with reckless abandon, are some of these possibilities.

Hymns

It is virtually impossible to join in the singing of a hymn on Sunday morning without culling from it a variety of sermon topics. For instance, I love to sing "Immortal, Invisible, God Only Wise" because of the third verse: "We blossom and flourish as leaves on the tree, and wither and perish—but naught changeth Thee." What a glorious theme about the constancy of God vis-à-vis human frailties. What would the sermon title (if you base it only on the above verse) be? How about "Here Today—Here Tomorrow"?

The second verse in this same hymn starts with "Unresting, unhasting, and silent as light." How about the sermon title as "Steady as She Goes"? This, of course, is a nautical term, which can be used to indicate the steady cruising of a ship very much like the steadiness of God which is available to us.

I recently joined in the singing of "If Thou but Suffer God to Guide Thee" and was struck by the last words of the last verse: "God never yet forsook at need the soul that trusted Him indeed." Several sermon titles jumped into mind, such as "Road Maps for Blind Faith" and "Big Brother, Little Brother," suggesting God's guidance in the first title and God's care in the second.

We've all sung "A Mighty Fortress Is Our God" hundreds of times. For some strange reason, the last time I sang it the hymn's several references to the Devil seemed to jump out and I thought of our Savior's several encounters with this being. You'll remember in the first verse: "For still our ancient foe doth seek to work us woe." In the third verse he crops up again with the mention of "The prince of darkness grim, we tremble not for him." I'd not heard much about the Devil in recent sermons. Did a title jump to mind? You bet: "The Devil and Dr. Jekyll." Robert Louis Stevenson's *Dr. Jekyll and Mr. Hyde* is one of literature's great classics because of its insight into man's duality. Isn't there a sermon on this subject about the tug-of-war in each of us just begging to be preached?

One statement caused me to start paying closer attention to the words in hymns. A woman remarked, "I used to sing the words in hymns mechanically. They seemed to have a certain rhythm to them, but they never really meant anything to me." The woman went on to explain that she experienced a long-lasting personal tragedy. Suddenly, every word in every verse of every hymn seemed to be written just for her.

You can build an entire sermon around a hymn. With an eye for provocative titling, you might announce that your next sermon will be "The Greatest Hymn Ever Written." Perhaps such a title would move less-than-enthusiastic congregants to attend church that Sunday. Without naming the hymn, you could open your sermon with remarks about the timeliness, the depth, and yet the appealing warmth of the words. You could cite the insight of the composer and his obvious deep faith, which we all seem to seek. After some degree of anticipation had been built up, you could announce that the hymn is "Amazing Grace." The exhortation of the sermon could then be the need for witnessing (as the hymn writer is doing) and its potential for leading souls to Christ. This hymn is reputed to have done more "soul saving" than any other, hence its claims to greatness. And of course many phrases within that hymn are potential sermon topics in themselves.

Hymns are generally masterpieces of coherency. Their writers don't try to cover a dozen topics at one writing but usually make them one-point messages. Listen carefully—and analytically—the next time you sing one. You'll notice that hymns, like psalms, back up their single points with concrete details that are pungently phrased topics in themselves.

Prose and Poetry

The world of literature is filled with good potential sermon topics. I was impressed recently by rereading one of Ralph Waldo Emerson's pieces, which went, in part, like this: "Finish every day and be done with it. You have done what you could. Some blunders and absurdities no doubt crept in; forget them as soon as you can." He went on to say, "This day is all that is good and fair. It is too dear, with its hopes and invitations, to waste a moment on the yesterday."

What a beautiful way to suggest that we try to live our lives one day at a time! Emerson sees the needlessness of worry over failures. To trust in God each day—and to do our best each day, as simplistic as that may sound—is the keystone to successful living.

One of my favorite poems is "The Chambered Nautilus" by Oliver Wendell Holmes. The last stanza goes:

> Build thee more stately mansions, O my soul,
> As the swift seasons roll!
> Leave thy low-vaulted past!
> Let each new temple, nobler than the last,
> Shut thee from heaven with a dome more vast,
> Till thou at length art free,
> Leaving thine outgrown shell by life's unresting sea!

The point here is the broadening, the widening, and the deepening of our character as we become more involved with the Christian ethic until finally we leave behind all that stood in the way of becoming one in Christ.

Another favorite is the closing stanza (it looks like I'm hooked on closing stanzas) of William Cullen Bryant's "Thanatopsis":

> So live, that when thy summons comes to join
> The innumerable caravan which moves
> To that mysterious realm, where each shall take
> His chamber in the silent halls of death,
> Thou go not, like the quarry-slave at night,
> Scourged to his dungeon, but, sustained and soothed
> By an unfaltering trust, approach thy grave
> Like one that wraps the drapery of his couch
> About him, and lies down to pleasant dreams.

Here we have sermonic application to the reasoning behind living the good life which ultimately prepares us for death.

One last example of poetry—and this one may not seem relevant at first to sermonizing—is a real favorite: "Sea-Fever" by John Masefield. Here it's the first verse (rather than the last) that is most memorable:

> I must go down to the seas again, to the lonely sea and the sky,
> And all I ask is a tall ship and a star to steer her by;
> And the wheel's kick and the wind's song and the white sail's shaking,
> And a gray mist on the sea's face, and a gray dawn breaking.

You might ask what that theme has to do with the church and the gospel. Read it again and again, and see Masefield's insatiable longing to get back to his first love, the sea. I understand his yearning; I feel closer to heaven on earth when walking on a beach than at any other place in this mortal life. Besides this love of the sea, I see a pulling, a gnawing to confront—to be with—something akin to a first love. I see a Christian who is drawn to the church: to serve it, to be a part of it, to sacrifice for it, to ultimately see its Founder and its Master. I see a Christian fever that produces restlessness, a hunger for companionship with God, and a calling that will not be denied. In a sermon inspired by this poem you could elaborate upon, and make as your theme, the magnetism pulling someone who has tasted the joys of Christ, just as Masefield knows the joys of being on the beloved sea again. Have I gone off the deep end on this one? I'm trying to indicate how the intensity of feeling in one area can lead to similar feelings in other areas for purposes of sermonizing.

Here are just the titles of three other poems, each of which is heavily freighted with suitable topics. Look them up, and you'll be able to recognize potential topics. They are: "Elegy Written in a Country Churchyard" by Thomas Gray, "In a Rose Garden" by John Bennett, and "Pioneers! O Pioneers!" by Walt Whitman.

Book Titles

One of my favorite Methodist minister friends was Dr. Carl Sanders, who was minister of Centenary United Methodist Church in Richmond, then superintendent of that denomination's Norfolk District, and retired as a bishop of the church. He was one of the greatest topical preachers I've ever heard.

One day I came across him in the book department of one of our leading department stores, where he appeared to be rummaging through the paperback section. As I came upon him I noticed in his hand a book on whose cover was a semi-draped woman in a rather provocative pose. Since Dr. Sanders was a down-to-earth sort of guy, I teased him a bit. "Caught in the act! But don't worry, Dr. Sanders, your secret is safe with me; I won't report you to your congregation for indulging in this kind of literature."

He let forth one of his marvelous robust laughs and said, "Don't worry, Hank, I don't read them. I just look on the covers to get sermon topic ideas." Then, rather excitedly, he pointed to the book in his hand. "See?" he exclaimed. "Take a look at this one."

I looked. As best I can remember, the title was something like "Unrequited Love." He went on to point out that these book titles provided an unlimited source of sermon topics. Before we parted company, he had lifted three or four more popular paperbacks off the shelf to prove his point. Suffice it to say, Dr. Sanders's sermon topics were always provocative, and his sermons were correspondingly intriguing.

During the 1982 Christmas shopping season, I was in a bookstore looking for books as gifts. I made some selections and, in waiting to pay the cashier, looked down at a table on which were several copies of a modern novel entitled *A Rose in Winter* by Kathleen Woodiwiss. I have no idea what the book was about, but the title startled me. I could envision a sermon with that title covering the subject of the bleakness, the desperation, the despair experienced by us humans when we get into the doldrums—the Dr. Zhivago-type of winter bitterness. Then comes the rescue from this winter of discontent by the shining, warm figure and spirit of Christ, the Rose in winter. All this came just from glancing at a book title. You can easily develop this same awareness and go up one bookshelf and down another—in any store or library—never running out of topic ideas. Don't appropriate these titles word for word, but with the use of some creativity and imagination, you will see scriptural application in many of them.

Radio and Television

It is hard to listen to the radio or watch television without spotting possible sermon topics. For instance, one evening the six o'clock news included an interview with a labor union member who said, "I was expecting a more positive position on the part of our union because we have supported our leaders to the hilt; we've paid our dues."

That last phrase, "We've paid our dues," set me to thinking about the theme of what constitutes a dues-paying member of a church. What does one have to "pay" to be looked upon as a genuine Christian in the eyes of God? Are there too many people who believe that outward participation—their works— are enough? This, of course, raises the ageless question of works vs. faith. In short, what are "dues," how much are they, and have we paid them?

In another instance, a United States senator made the statement on television that he was worried about this country's solvency. Immediately, a sermon title came to mind: "How Solvent Are You?" Or how about "Our State of Solvency"? Here you can think at once about our worth to the church. Is our account on the church books in a solvent condition? Is our participation in faith and our support of the church's program substantial enough to be considered in the black? Or are we phlegmatic Christians to the point that we are "in the red"— insolvent?

Television newscasters employ a slick method of holding your attention by encouraging you to stay tuned via a device called a grabber. This is a two- or three-word condensation of the next news item or items to follow. A recent one said "Sealed Orders from the White House." Immediately I thought, "Go ye into all the world and preach the gospel to every creature." This admonition may not be a "sealed" order but, like such an order, it projects an aura of vital importance. And it may remind you of other biblical "orders," which, without excessive pontificating, will make interesting topics.

Another recent grabber said "Looking for Bargains." This had to do with the current economic situation, but a counterphrase jumped to mind which you've heard many times: "When Is a Bargain a Bargain?" This led me to think at once of the old standby "You Get What You Pay For." This led me to think further about the "bargain" we find in the Christian church, the biggest bargain of all. We must subscribe unequivocally to John 3:16 and lead the type of life that should follow this understanding and belief—all of which means we will have everlasting life. Great ideas can come out of a quick phrase flashed on the television screen.

Newspapers and Magazines

In your daily reading, you will also come upon phrases that will stir an imagination trained to be alert to their possible use. Take the simple notice that has become an integral part of Americana: YARD SALE. As you know, anyone can participate in this kind of commerce. Everybody's trying, as Jimmy Durante said years ago, to get into the act. Aren't there a lot of things (habits, disbeliefs, cynicism, despair, malice, greed) we should try to get rid of? Why not have a spiritual yard sale? Get rid of the junk and in its place put those things that should be substituted. Be most selective about what you put back into the limited space available.

I'm an omnivorous magazine reader—in the sense that I flip through magazines quickly; I've still not found the time to indulge in total reading. The chart summarizes suggestions found in two magazines picked up at random: one magazine through its articles, the other through its advertisements.

Smithsonian, **April 1985 (articles only)**

Article Title	*Article Theme*	*Sermon Title and Topic*
He Makes Guitars for the Stars	Danny Ferrington's custom-made musical instruments	"How to Create a Masterpiece": The roughness of human material—ordinary people God uses to create saints
Vision Is More than Meets the Eye	The physiological process of sight	"Now You See It, Now You Don't": Pentecost Sunday; the birth and inflow of the invisible but omnipresent Holy Spirit—around us, today and forever
The "Ghost Army" That Helped Defeat Germany	The U.S. outfit that used dummy tanks, phony troops, elaborate ruses	"Telling the Real from the Unreal": distinguishing the true, lasting precepts and creations of God from the ephemeral contrivances and forms of humankind
The Man Who Mined Musical Gold in Appalachia	How Cecil Sharp turned out folk-song classics	"Attention All Prospectors": Cite Russell Conwell's "Acres of Diamonds"; don't limit your horizons, but don't neglect treasures and opportunities for service around us—family, friends, church, etc.

The New Yorker, June 10, 1985 (advertisements only)

Ad Title	Name of Product	Sermon Title and Topic
Aren't You Glad You Never Slowed Down?	British Airways	"The Stamina of the Good Guys": In running the Christian race there are always unexpected, supportive strengths—and victory is sweet
What Should *You Expect* from a Working "Partnership" with Hewlett-Packard?	Hewlett-Packard computer systems	"Looking for a Prosperous Partnership?": The assured joys—strength, love, peace, knowledge, salvation—through a "partnership" with Christ
The Grand Little Hotel of Chicago	The Barclay	"Four-Star Hotel": "In my Father's house are many mansions"—the ultimate goal for Christians
"Of Course I'm Sure, I Read It in *Business Week*	*Business Week* magazine	"The Unbiased Referee": The clarity of the Bible, its unequivocal position on matters for living—and dying

Religion

The best source of all sermon material is the Bible itself. The book of Proverbs is an especially fascinating source of titles. But Psalms, Ecclesiastes—indeed, almost every book of the Bible—contain striking turns of phrase that make good sermon topics. Try looking at unfamiliar translations of the Bible for fresh ideas along this line.

Another source from the area of religion is the startling sentences from the sermons of other ministers. For instance, Jerry Falwell in a television broadcast described the tenacity of a certain individual as one "who would charge hell with a bucket of water."

Miscellaneous

This is the potpourri section: random thoughts on random subjects. Here's a rambling list of topics recorded when the thought struck me.

"Lover's Quarrel." This comes from the phrase Robert Frost requested be engraved on his tombstone: "I had a lover's quarrel with the world." Have you had a lover's quarrel with the church or with Christ? Your Christian strength undoubtedly caused a happy settlement.

"The Most Dangerous Prayer Imaginable." This possibility jumped into my mind during an evening walk when I was repeating the Lord's Prayer. Wouldn't I be in one royal mess if God forgave my debts the way in which I forgive my debtors? This would be a wonderful base for a sermon on forgiveness.

"A Glorious State of Affairs." I thought of this while I was going over the last line of the Twenty-third Psalm: "and I shall dwell in the house of the Lord for ever." This is what I call a "dessert" or "frosting" subject. It's especially good following one or more sermons making reference to the halcyonic, magnificent life awaiting the true believer. It can be a description of God's kingdom.

"The Deadest Place in the World." A friend asked me to carry some photographs to church; it was difficult for us to get together during the week. I put them in an envelope, placed them beside me in the pew—and forgot to pick them up and take them to our usual coffee hour. When I saw my friend, it suddenly occurred to me that I'd left the photographs in the pew. The sexton hadn't yet made his rounds, so when I got back to the sanctuary, there they were where I had sat. No one else was in the church. I stood for a moment, reflecting on the silence and remembering the glorious anthems and the wonderful hymn-singing and the fine sermon I'd heard just a few moments ago. But now the place was like a tomb. Then it struck me: "After the tumult and the shouting had died, and the captains and the kings had departed," this sanctuary ostensibly was a dead place. How much of what had transpired moments ago would be taken out of this building and put into daily living? Had the lessons learned died with the passing of this short period of time?

"Old Chinese Proverbs." I have long been an afficionado of old sayings. There are few—if any—to shoot holes through. Take two, for instance: "Don't cross the bridge before you come to it" and "Don't holler before you're hurt." Both seem

to tie into a New Testament theme: Don't worry about tomorrow, remember the lilies of the field. If I were putting a sermon together on this subject, I'd tell about the last time I was in a Chinese restaurant and read with anticipation the sayings printed on the paper slips in fortune cookies. I like to compare the wisdom from this source over against the Christian "wisdom." Don't laugh, just save your fortune cookie slips; you'll be amazed at some of their possibilities.

"Is Your Pass Valid?" A newspaper notice told of the coming of a soloist to appear with our city's symphony orchestra. The body of the article said, "Those holding valid season passes will be given first choice of reservations." I began to wonder if my "pass" (my faith) was good enough to get me into the kingdom. What does one do to earn such a pass? Is my pass, indeed, valid?

"Museum Quality Reproductions." An ad about a group of limited edition collectibles stressed the fact that these items were not just ordinary reproductions but, rather, were of museum quality and would stand close examination. My immediate thought: Is my life a reproduction of Christ's and, if so, of what quality is this reproduction? Will my life—my brand of Christianity—also stand close inspection?

"Back to Square One." This phrase has become hackneyed, but everyone seems to use it when there are indications that a new starting point is needed, especially when a project has gotten off to a bad start. In sermonic terms we can use the analogy of the prodigal son, who finally "got back to square one." Generally, "square one" indicates the true, unblemished, unquestioned set of principles that should be used as a starting point. "Square one" in the Christian life can be Christ, the Bible, the church, or any combination of these basic elements of our religion.

"Smuggling Dawn Past a Rooster." This was part of a sentence (I believe in a play) in which a cynic said, "Keeping this plan secret is like trying to smuggle dawn past a rooster." At the time I thought of God's omnipresence, alertness, watchfulness (and please forgive the unfortunate comparison of God to a rooster). I was thinking of the untiring vigilance of a God who is never caught napping.

"Don't Rain on My Parade." This line from a Streisand song has reached a point of popularity. I've heard it used when plans and dreams have gone awry. You know, of course, what comes to mind. The "parade" was our earthly journey, and sometimes unfortunate things befall us. These turn out to be the "rain." But how do Christians look upon rain on their parade? Take it from there.

"But You Can Go Home." This observation is counter to Thomas Wolfe's "You can't go home again." Indicate the "home" that awaits the repentant person who feels life is aimless and without purpose. There is a home for everyone, which is the Christian church. Does this remind you of the story of the Prodigal Son?

"To Make a Long Story Short...." Another saying, another sermon topic. This might be a good topic for Easter or Christmas, both of which are long stories that can be made short when their recounting indicates the purposes behind the birth and resurrection of Christ.

"Hide and Seek." There's nothing new about this phrase, but I did see its use in a recent Raytheon ad describing its electronic system for aircraft and naval vessels. The caption was "How We Help the Air Force Hide While It Seeks." Immediately I thought of the way in which we hide (avoid) the kingdom and Christ's love but how Christ can seek us out and find us.

"Class Reunion." When I attended a school class reunion, this phrase came to mind as a sermon possibility: specifically, the similarity between my secular class reunion and the "class reunion" I hope to participate in later on when I might be privileged to meet some of the saints—and some of my friends —who have preceded me into heaven.

A recent *Wall Street Journal* ran an article about offbeat sources of learning for employees of Bell Telephone Laboratories. On one occasion they spent an afternoon at a lecture entitled "150 Years of Bridge Building." Other studies included such topics as "Learning to Fly" and "The Mystery of Bird Navigation." These lectures were known as "general research colloquia." No one worried that such topics had little to do with communications research, because the purpose was to generate ideas. In the same way, you don't have to closet yourself in your study or stare at religious pictures or listen to sacred music to get sermon topic ideas.

Constant Awareness

Let's clear up one point that may be bothering you: Don't think for a minute that your preaching ministry should be built around flash-in-the-pan ideas that jump to mind from some of these sources simply because you develop a sensitivity to their potential use. Rather, a continuing awareness of the numerous subjects that overwhelm us daily may very well have a direct relation to doctrinal or topical preaching. These sources can provide a refreshing way of stating a Christian principle you feel deeply and would like to preach about. A favorite scripture may be evoked by the mere suggestion of the phrase to which you are exposed. Such a scripture, obviously, can then be used as the sermon topic.

As for one entire sermon inspiring another sermon by virtue of its topic, try to come up with a more provocative title than this one: "Rob Any Churches Lately?" This was a sermon by Presbyterian minister Fred Swearingen and, if you haven't guessed it by now, had to do with stewardship. He relied on Malachi's "Will man rob God?" For you, as a minister or theological student, this might be just one more catchy title. For me, as a layman, however, wild horses couldn't have kept me away from a sermon with a title like that, and a truly magnificent sermon it was. Another of his sermons was titled simply "Here and Now," but the bulletin for that day showed that its subtitle was "On the Problem of Being Somewhere Else When It's Happening Here." And still another of his titles, for a sermon immediately following Christmas: "Too Much Stable? Too Much Star?"

An outstanding sermon whose title is a masterpiece of creativity was "Two Bad Boys and a Party," delivered by one of my pastors, Ben Sparks. I went to hear that sermon thinking the two bad boys might be Cain and Abel. Or were they Esau and Jacob? No, one of the boys was the Prodigal Son and the other was his brother. The Prodigal Son was "bad" because he ran away from home and indulged himself in riotous living, while the other boy was "bad" because of his uncharitable reception of the returning brother who had been considered lost. Both the Swearingen and the Sparks sermons are good examples of imaginative titling.

I'll leave you with three last points about this subject: First, the world is bulging with potential sermon subjects: Stop—look—listen. Second, jot down on a piece of paper potential sermon titles as soon as possible after they strike you or you'll probably forget them. If the idea comes from a magazine or newspaper, tear out the section (if practicable) to keep these ideas for either the sermon topic or for a supporting point in a sermon. Then classify them by headings for future reference. Do the same type of cataloging for anecdotes (see chapter 17 on humor). Third, does a flavorless title indicate a flavorless sermon? Many people think so. I know I do.

3

Strengthening the Structure of the Sermon

After the sermon topic has been selected, one of the most important points to remember is that the preacher will be trying to communicate through a barrier. The word "barrier" may be strong, but it is purposely chosen to illustrate the difficulty facing ministers in trying to communicate their trained and experienced theological conclusions to those who often put ministers in an exalted position simply because they are ministers. This inbred "reverence" fostered through the ages will, I daresay, continue indefinitely. The humanity of ministers is often more difficult to perceive than that of lay people. It takes skill to bridge this gap, to talk things over or converse with congregants rather than to pontificate. This challenge should be kept in mind not only in delivery style but in the structure of the sermon itself.

Few things are more refreshing than to hear a preacher augment sermon points by quoting *recent* happenings, such as "I heard on the radio just yesterday that . . ." or "When I took the newspaper off the porch this morning I noticed on the front page that . . ." This indicates a high degree of alertness—the sermon topic was so much on the minister's mind that the corollary was instantly recognized—and gives the sermon subject a fresh and up-to-date flavor, a truly *current* emphasis.

Use Personal Experiences

Nothing quite provides credibility in making a point as well as a personal experience. "I was in the Dallas airport one stormy day last summer waiting for planes to get back on schedule and struck up a conversation with another equally impatient traveler in an adjacent seat in the terminal lobby. He began telling me about the delays it seemed he must face in every area of his business and personal life. 'Is life supposed to be like that?' he asked me."

If such a chance meeting does happen to you, and out of it comes an experience mirroring a Christian principle, your use of it as an example will reinforce an interesting sermon point.

The very fact that you were there—that you tasted, felt, saw, or heard the experience—removes the possibility of exaggeration brought about by secondhand recounting of a story. Most people are aware of the tendency toward exaggeration when someone says, "He told me he had met this stranger in the Dallas airport who raised the question . . ." In the first-person case, you have unshakable credentials.

Ben Sparks told in a sermon about his growing up in a church where the Women of the Church organization took turns driving an elderly lady to some of the poorer sections of the city to distribute gifts to the indigent. Ben said that when he became sixteen years of age and got his driver's license, he did some of the driving. While he had "Bible-learning" about the need to help the poor, this exposed him for the first time to the plight of these unfortunates, and, he said, he'd never forgotten it. The experience helped him preach on the subject. And when he preached on the subject, I listened with respect to his words because I knew he had been there. This was a firsthand telling.

Obviously, you shouldn't invent an experience and claim that it is true. But you can dig deeply into your memory and make a valiant effort to recall any exposure you may have had that can be associated with each of your sermon topics to achieve this firsthand credibility.

Identify Quote Sources

Ministers often augment their points by quoting persons of unquestioned stature in their fields. This is fine and should be done where appropriate. It gives the minister the added comfort of implying, I'm not the only one who takes this position; somebody wiser than both of us thought the same thing.

But bear in mind that many in your congregation are not learned people. There is inevitably a mix within every church, regardless of the general socioeconomic level or even the neighborhood in which the church is located.

One time I heard a minister insert in his sermon, "As James Barrie said, 'Those who bring sunshine to the lives of others cannot keep it from themselves.'" This was an appropriate quotation for that sermon, but I'm sure many people were wondering, "Who is James Barrie?" You and I (readers that we are) know of course that Barrie was the renowned Scottish novelist and dramatist, author of *Peter Pan.* But how about those who did not know?

Take another example: A minister included these words in his sermon: "And as John A. Symonds wrote:

. . . but God abides and in man's heart
Speaks with the clear unconquerable cry
Of energies and hopes that cannot die."

How many listeners realized that John A. Symonds was a nineteenth-century English scholar?

One minister quoted some chap named Bill Bertner; in the same sermon he also quoted a Peggy Nash. If any reader can identify either of these people, I would certainly like to know who they were. Their back-up would have meant more with proper identification.

Cut and Compact

There are, no doubt, a few preachers who would do well to respect George Eliot's observation, "Blessed are they who have nothing to say and cannot be persuaded to say it." Given the fact that something must be said, there have always been proponents of brevity in the pulpit. This isn't to say that brief sermons are necessarily profound; I've heard weak sermons that were mercifully brief. It is important, however, to keep sermons within a reasonable time span.

After the sermon is composed, the fat must be cut off and the balance compacted into a tight but skillfully delivered message. As the American poet Marianne Craig Moore put it, "Expanded explanation tends to spoil the lion's leap."

In his fine book on preaching entitled *Be Brief About It,* Robert D. Young pointed out that the first step to relevant preaching is to be conscious of time and to realize that something weighty must be said in a set period. The very idea of brevity, he wrote, conjures up crisp words, tight language, orderly argument, deft illustration. Note his use of the adjectives "crisp," "tight," "orderly," and "deft." All these, if used properly, indicate a good start down the road of organizing a fine sermon.

Several years ago, my mother sent me a poem that highlights what we have been saying.

> I have only just a minute,
> Only sixty seconds in it,
> Forced upon me, don't refuse it,
> Didn't seek it, didn't choose it,
> But it's up to me to use it,
> I must suffer if I abuse it.
> Just a tiny little minute
> But eternity is in it.

Observing Reactions

Through the years, it's been my habit to observe people's reactions to various activities. When I earned money for college by ushering in a movie theater, I soon learned that the best show was not on the screen but in the audience. After watching snatches of a given movie for a week, I learned which portions of the story usually caused the strongest audience reaction, be it laughter, tears, giggling, gasps, or what have you. To check out the audience reaction, I would walk down the aisle just in advance of one of these movie highlights, turn around, and head back up the aisle for a "front-row seat" in watching its impact.

This habit lives with me today. I find myself on museum tours watching the facial expressions of those persons looking at works of art. When I had time to go to football and baseball games, I watched the faces of those who were watching. I've done the same thing at business meetings and conferences. And I always sit in the rear of a theater or in a meeting. That way, the back-row seat becomes a "front-row" seat. I can observe without being obvious.

This habit has gone with me to church. While listening to the sermon—and I do pay close attention to it—I let my eyes wander across the congregation to check reaction. When the sermon reaches a magical twenty-minute point, I start to notice, almost inevitably, the crossing and uncrossing of legs, the shifting about in the pews, the gazing upward toward the ceiling, the clearing of the throats, and so on. The exception is when the sermon is excellent and it's so quiet that you could hear the proverbial pin drop. I hope that from this book you'll learn to create and deliver sermons so well that this will be commonplace for you.

How Long a Sermon?

This brings up the ideal length of time for a sermon. Unless the preacher has superb rhetorical skills, twenty minutes is about all that can be comfortably listened to. In most of the Protestant churches I've attended, the sermon is usually in the last half of the service. If the sermon is too strung-out, fatigue begins to set in. More important, the receptivity of the average churchgoer's mind appears to become exhausted outside the range of twenty minutes.

I use twenty minutes as the maximum time period because, on the one hand, it is impractical to develop and deliver a subject in less time than that. On the other hand, we find fatigue working its way through the congregation. And we must remember that congregants are usually aware when a sermon is getting too long.

You properly raise the question, "But twenty minutes isn't enough time to develop this or that subject; I'll be doing it an injustice. After all, these people are only here one hour a week, and I can't skimp and cut just to conform to some well-worn custom of 'get 'em in and get 'em out.'"

It Can Be Cut

For several years one of my responsibilities with a large corporation was to summarize appeals for contributions from charitable organizations that were to be considered at our monthly Board of Directors meeting. After having performed exhaustive studies of such appeals, I was shocked to learn in the early stages of this assignment that such a presentation had to be condensed on one sheet of paper. It seemed impossible. But it had to be done, out of deference to the few valuable minutes the board set aside for this purpose. And I did it, although it required, in any number of cases, the summarizing of some seven or eight pages of single-spaced typed material onto that single sheet.

You may say that's fine, but certain sermon topics cannot be properly covered in twenty minutes. *Any* topic can be covered within that time. As one preacher friend told me, "If I can't reach them in twenty minutes, I'd better quit, because I can see them starting to squirm." Later in this chapter I'll give you my outline for a sermon I was asked to preach on the subject of the stewardship of time, which started out to be fifty minutes long! There was no way I could cover that subject in twenty minutes—but I did.

One Sunday I had the flu, so I stayed home and listened to our service on the radio. The twenty-minute sermon went by so fast! If I had coughed much, I would have missed some salient points.

On that Sunday it occurred to me: Is this twenty-minute exposure what a seven-year college stint is all about—studying, among other things, homiletics? If so, there are no more stringent requirements placed on anyone, regardless of profession. Our minister, I concluded on that eye-opening day, has a whale of a job to do in a very short space of time.

Out of that experience also came the realization that preachers must hone and craft each word as if it were jealous of being crowded in by strange words. And, for the sake of time economy, preachers must plan to use only those words that will not prove to be excess baggage.

The Strength of Simple Words

One way to strengthen the structure of any sermon is to use words so simple and clear that they—and the entire sermon—will be thoroughly understood. Even technical information can be explained simply. When my family doctor comes forth with all sorts of medical terms and evaluations, I usually ask him, "What does that mean in French?" At the corner garage, when something's wrong with my car, I learn about strange parts I had no idea had been implanted in Detroit.

The value of speaking so you can be understood was demonstrated some years ago by a distinguished chemist who was about to give a lecture on heavy water. Sensing that he had persons of different educational levels and competence in the audience, he announced, "I am going to divide this lecture into two parts; the first will be a popular treatment of the subject, the second will be specialized and technical. When I finish the first part, I shall stop for a brief intermission so that those of you who are not interested in my calculations and charts will not be bored stiff but may leave." The audience appreciated his thoughtfulness, and he was rewarded by receiving spirited questions from those who remained through the second part.

Each profession or trade has its own language. The physician is certainly a novice at theology and would be unable to follow a discussion on eschatology. The engineer has little, if any, knowledge of the law; the word "tort" would probably be baffling. The business man or woman may know the market and the product but is puzzled and annoyed (to go back to my example of my family doctor) by words like "suture" and "sump." This also applies to the special language of theologians. Many words and expressions learned at the seminary are needed to clarify and understand biblical interpretation. But for lay people, the minister should remove all mystery from a technical word or phrase learned while struggling for that D. Min. degree.

I've heard in sermons such words and phrases as: Pentateuch, Canon of the Bible, Ezra reading from the Torah, and the Septuagint version of a particular law. And there were looks of puzzlement (I checked the faces of several who were listening closely) when the preacher said, "Some wisdom in this area was reputedly found in the Apocrypha, which of course was not accepted as authentic."

Secular Communication Barriers

In my early days in public relations, I trained tour guides whose duties were to escort visitors through various buildings, most of which housed complex equipment. At first, I let these guides compose their own ten-minute narratives, on the theory that this would give them a sense of proprietorship in telling their own story. I was devastated by their use of highly technical terms obviously not understandable to visitors.

With much cajoling, I tried to convince them to substitute simpler, nontechnical words, but I didn't have much success. I finally had to be firm. This admonition did the trick: If what you say can be understood by a thirteen-year-old, consider yourself a success. It worked. Guests leaving these tours were requested to write their comments in a visitors' book at the exit stations. Aside from other compliments, their remarks usually made a grateful reference to the understandability of the guides' narrations.

How Large Is Your Vocabulary?

The average person has a limited vocabulary for everyday use, a more ample one for writing, and a considerably larger vocabulary for reading. People have a general understanding of many words they often see in print but never use in conversation. They seldom take the trouble to learn the exact meaning, the pronunciation, and the common usage. Sometimes they are fascinated by a new word because it seems to be more descriptive than any they've learned thus far, but they are afraid they will sound strange or affected if they use it.

As a result, they stick to a feeble and poverty-stricken vocabulary of a few hundred words, even though a little effort would provide several thousand words that are normally at the command of every well-educated man and woman.

Use short, simple words if they prove to be adequate. If you find yourself leaning toward a larger, multisyllabic word because you feel it is more descriptive or precise, it may be appropriate to use it. This is a judgmental factor that must be applied as circumstances dictate. If ever in doubt, go the simpler route of the short word. Chances are you won't be misunderstood.

Pretentiousness can also unwittingly invade a sermon. It is certainly in bad taste to dress up one's language with this silly quality. For instance, there are some people who never go to bed; they always "retire." They don't get up, they "rise." In their language, nobody ever dies, they "pass on." Don't think that common words are too common. Chances are they will express the bulk of your meaning. They are necessary, honest, and direct. They are glorified by Shakespeare and the Bible. Franklin, Emerson, and Lincoln all had a spirited and eloquent speech usually made up of simple words. By using such words, you can say what you really think, not what you think you ought to say, or what another person or a book would say.

Activate and Energize

Most speakers naturally place high priority on the need to provide information in any public talk. I look upon the sermon pretty much in the same way. But both a public talk and a sermon are ineffective if the main purpose of each is solely to provide the listener with information. This can be a sermon's glaring shortcoming. It is all too easy to leave the congregation hanging after an otherwise fine sermon. People need to know what they are supposed to do with the subject matter.

A good friend told me that she wants to be moved into action by sermons. One Sunday she said, "That was a beautiful message today, but I don't know what to do about it, except to hope, or love—or something elusive like that." She went on to say that those things are too indefinite, too loose, for her. My response was that certain sermons can move you into measurable church work such as visiting shut-ins or aiding the poor. But there are unavoidable areas of what appear to be physical inaction such as love, hope, and salvation. Some of these intangibles can move us into definitive action; for instance, in the area of prayer. I'm not sure she fully subscribed to my reasoning. But—at least in my own mind—prayer is action.

A lot of people, including this woman, don't want to hear a theological treatise Sunday after Sunday, researched and delivered in a scholarly manner, to the exclusion of some "how-to"s for personal living. Many of them face severe problems and need more pragmatic approaches to life in the face of their frustrations and disappointments. All this isn't to suggest that "theological" sermons be entirely avoided—or even minimized—but they shouldn't become a steady diet.

As George E. Sweazey so aptly said in his *Preaching the Good News*, "Many an otherwise important sermon is left hanging in mid-air because the preacher never connects it with real living. Preaching is never intended to give the hearers some information and leave them where they were before." I look upon a minister as a servant of God who was inspired and then trained to guide me in making decisions about my Christian life. And from Sunday to Sunday, I expect the sermon to tell me what to do, what action I should take. But something—give me *something* to do with that sermon!

Does a Sermon Change Church Members?

Every minister or theological student should keep two 3-by-5 cards permanently in the study. Write the word BEFORE in large letters on one card, and write the word AFTER on the other. Prop up the first card somewhere on the desk during the composition of your sermon. Glance at it frequently as a reminder of the suspected nature of certain congregants who conceivably might be helped by the sermon message. After the sermon is composed, cover the BEFORE card with the AFTER card. Obviously the question arises: Will the church member be the same after the sermon is delivered as before? If your honest answer is affirmative, you'd better take another look at the treatment of the sermon, if only at the conclusion (for the importance of the conclusion see chapter 7).

A recent article by a direct marketing expert pointed out that the objective of advertising isn't to amuse or entertain. It's to inform, to persuade, to sell. He said, "That kind of advertising never wins a popularity contest. Only a sales contest." (And you know what the "product" is that the average minister has to "sell.") This article listed twenty-one skills to be employed in writing the typical sales letter that accompanies literature kits and brochures. The twenty-first point was:

> End your letter by telling the reader exactly what he should do, when he should do it, how he should do it, and what he stands to lose if he doesn't do it. The reader of such a letter is activated and energized.

Which Part First?

Workshop conferences and books on preaching give varied answers to the question of the order in which the sermon should be prepared. Most writers and speakers indicate that the main points—the body—should be tackled initially. Some experienced homileticians suggest that the introduction be prepared last. Others suggest that in any case the conclusion should be prepared first; after all, this is the point at which the congregation is left and is the goal for the entire sermon.

Follow Logical Order

If you want to go from A to E, the way to go is from A to B, C, D, and then E. Start at the beginning (introduction), work your way through the body message (the major points), and end with a conclusion that reminds the listener of the principal reason for the message in the first place. In making hundreds of public speeches—and several lay sermons—I found this approach much the best way to put my message together.

Many skilled speakers and preachers feel that the middle message—the main points—should be developed first to keep clean the total idea you want to get across. At this stage of preparation, they would be uncluttered by the introduction and conclusion. This is well and good, and if you feel more comfortable using this method, by all means use it. But remember that although I work on the introduction first, the subject —the purpose—of my talk or sermon has already been decided, even though the details haven't yet been refined.

On one occasion when asked to give a lay sermon, I chose a subject that had bothered me considerably. The point I wished to make involved the stewardship of time as covered by Jesus in the twenty-fifth chapter of Matthew. He was talking, you'll remember, about some of the unfortunate states of humanity when people were hungry, thirsty, strangers, sick, or in prison and no one came to their aid. I knew generally what I wanted to say, but I certainly didn't have the points of the message finalized. But why, even before the decision about my main points, should I be concerned with my introductory remarks? Let me draw a comparison.

If you've ever played baseball or softball, you'll understand the need to take a few practice swings and move the bat around to get the feel of actually being at the plate. You've seen professional baseball players go through all sorts of motions to get flexed up, physically and mentally, ranging from tugging at their hat brims to hitting the spikes of their shoes with their bats. Conversely, it's rare to see a batter stride up to the plate with his bat in hand, stand as stiff as a poker, and wait for the first pitch. There is, in short, an introduction he makes —or goes through—before his actual performance. Similarly, joggers realize the necessity of stretching exercises to prevent muscle damage before they begin to run. They don't just dash wildly out their front door and begin running around the block at full steam.

The next four chapters discuss the three inescapable divisions of the sermon—the introduction, main body, and conclusion—starting with the introduction, which I personally prefer to do first.

4

How to Construct
the Introduction

It's most important to understand how vital the sermon introduction is. First impressions are critical; they are often remembered long after everything else about the subject or experience is forgotten. According to the Theory of Primacy and Recency, known for years and recently confirmed and subscribed to by psychological testing, you will know that:

First position is the second most remembered   (Introduction)
Third position is remembered best   (Conclusion)
Second position is remembered least   (Body)

One of the greatest sermonic arts is to get the attention of the listener at the very outset. But how to do it?

Attention-Getting Questions

Asking a question demands an answer. If the question isn't too interesting or startling, the answer may be halfhearted, but at least there'll be one. So one way to get started is by asking a question, perhaps a somewhat startling one, to place the listener in the position where there is little choice but to come up with some kind of answer.

For instance, wouldn't you suddenly become more attentive to a sermon if the minister began by saying, "Suppose you were flying in a jet at thirty-six thousand feet over the Atlantic Ocean. Suddenly you felt a vibration in the plane, and you suspected something was wrong. Then you heard, over the loudspeaker, 'This is your captain speaking. We've developed a problem in one of our engines, but everything is under control, and I'm sure we'll make it to England.' Then, following that disquieting message, you started to see and smell smoke. My question is: What would be your first thoughts if you were in such a situation?"

It would be disastrous, of course, for the minister to plunge headlong into the rest of the sermon without waiting for a few moments to let the congregants come up with their answers to what is not an unreasonable question. The sermon then could take any number of tacks, such as belief in God's ordering of events, opportunities given Christians to revise their lives, the overarching providence of God during precarious moments. But at least the minister has gotten the audience involved at the outset.

Or, back to the earlier example of using Matthew 25:41–46, you might ask, "Have you ever been really hungry—I mean *really* hungry—not the hunger you experience from dieting but the painful physical hunger and mental anguish brought about by not knowing when you will get another meal? Or have you ever felt so alone that you knew no one in the world was aware of your existence—and you even doubted that God knew you were down here suffering with indescribable loneliness? Or have you ever been in prison, thrown in with people you considered to be the dregs of humanity, and felt your very soul split in two when you heard the steel door slam shut behind you?" After that opening, you might wait ten full seconds before uttering another word. There would be a powerful lot of thinking going on in the congregation.

Attention-Getting Statements

Aside from actually raising a question, there is the equally good opportunity of making a statement—a startling statement.

For instance: "I had left the hospital room for the third time that week after visiting a very old and close friend of mine who had been quite ill for almost a month. Frankly, I didn't know what was wrong. As I closed his hospital room door, I bumped into his doctor, whom by this time I had gotten to know. The doctor's expression told me that he recognized my grief and concern. I asked him, 'How long is it going to take before he will be up and around again? We certainly do miss him.' The doctor hesitated but then said, 'He's got terminal cancer.' "

One of my sons gave an example of this "startling statement" principle. He was in the barber shop one evening when an announcer's voice on television said excitedly, "A killer is loose in our midst!" Everyone in the shop stopped talking and turned toward the set. It turned out that the "killer" was cancer, and the announcement was of a public service nature. Nevertheless, it got attention.

Ordinary Incidents

Begin with an account to which the congregation can easily relate. For instance: "The other day I asked a bright young man who had just gotten his college diploma what he wanted to do with his life. He said that he wanted to be a television star, or a big league baseball player, or the owner of a large stable of horses. Actually, he didn't particularly care which of the three he ended up being, as long as he became very rich in the process."

This type of opening arrests attention at the outset because it involves a typical modern youth. From the preacher's standpoint, it opens any number of doors for content possibilities. I can see the title: "Rich Man, Poor Man." The sermon message would involve the things in life that make us truly rich and raise the point that a rich man can really be poor. Anyone can take off on that subject readily. But the point is that there was an element of attention-getting at the very outset.

Humor as a Springboard

There is also a place for humor in the introduction. It's dangerous to use this element without a reasonable degree of experience and skill. As chapter 17, on the subject of humor, points out, a preacher should not be a stand-up comic and turn the pulpit into a stage. Here are a few examples of the judicious use of humor in the introduction.

One Sunday in my church, Dr. Hartley Hall, president of Union Theological Seminary in Virginia, was the guest preacher. Our church's recently called minister, Ben Sparks, had returned that Sunday to his former church in Tennessee for the installation service of his successor. In his opening remarks Dr. Hall said, "I do not envy Mr. Sparks's trip to his former church. There is nothing quite so demoralizing to a minister as to visit his former congregation and find out that they are getting along perfectly well without him."

Another visitor to our pulpit was our former minister, Jim Anderson, who at this writing is minister of the Kirk-in-the-Hills

Presbyterian Church in Bloomfield Hills, Michigan. He hadn't been among us for several years. It was understandable that he wouldn't remember all of us by name. So he wisely began this way: "You'll please forgive me if I don't remember each of you as I once did. I'm reminded of the minister like me who returned to his former flock and was greeted by an old friend, a lady parishioner. He inquired about her husband and was told, 'He died and went to heaven.' The returning minister replied, 'Oh, I'm sorry to hear that.' Upon reflection, that didn't sound right so he amended it to 'Oh, I'm glad to hear that.' Then he thought that wasn't right and so he said, finally, 'I'm surprised to hear that.'"

Or if you're asked to fill the pulpit in another church on a given Sunday, you might borrow the following introductory remarks: "Please be charitable in your appraisal of my sermonic efforts. After all, I'm just here temporarily. I remember another supply minister who made those same remarks but carried them a bit further. He reminded the congregation that if a windowpane in the church were broken, a piece of cardboard could be placed in the opening until repair work was done. He explained that he was like that piece of cardboard, just a temporary measure. After the service, an enthusiastic lady approached him, saying, 'I thought you were simply marvelous, and I can't understand why you insisted upon comparing yourself to a piece of cardboard. As far as I was concerned, you were a real pane.'"

Whatever introductory method you prefer to use—the jolting question, the startling statement, the recollection of an ordinary event, the use of humor—it should be carefully planned. Regardless of your pulpit skill, don't leave the introduction to be handled at the last moment; don't downgrade it to a position below the rest of the sermon.

Connecting the Introduction with the Theme

At this all-important point in the construction of the introduction, we confront the unavoidable question of theme, from which the homiletician who respects the hearing and understanding abilities of the congregation cannot run. There is a beautiful statement that defies improvement, although it is as old as the hills. Every person who has studied speaking or preaching has heard it. But it is so fundamentally sound that I would be derelict not to include it. It involves the question asked of the unpolished but venerated rural preacher, "How come your sermons are always so good?" He responded, "First, I tell 'em what I'm going to tell 'em; then I tell 'em; then I tell em' what I told 'em." Let's call these the Perfect Preaching Principles. I'll use each of them as the focus of the three divisions of the sermon: the introduction, the body, and the conclusion.

Now that we're at the point of reviewing our possible techniques to get the congregation's attention, we must tie the attention-getter to the theme of the sermon by using the first Preaching Principle of "telling 'em what you're going to tell 'em."

Judgment must be used here to relate these two elements. Going back to the examples of the past several pages, we find that a question asked by the preacher can lead into this position statement. For example:

What would you do in that jet at thirty-six thousand feet? You will notice that the question at the end of that attention-getter was, "What would be your first thoughts if you were in such a situation?" I would then say something like, "That's what I want to talk about this morning: the strength of our belief—of our faith—in times of peril."

In the second example involving Matthew 25 and made up entirely of questions, I might "tell 'em what I'm going to tell 'em" with the statement, "Let's examine this morning one of the real meanings of Christian service when this service takes the form of direct, tangible aid to a suffering humanity."

In the third example of my having left the hospital room of a sick friend as the doctor informed me of his terminal illness, I might use as my "telling 'em what I'm going to tell 'em" statement, "Let's talk today about the impact of grief, especially when it comes to us, as it often does, in the form of a shock. What do we do, where do we go, to see this grief mitigated?"

In the case of the young man who wanted to make it big in television, the big leagues, or as a horse owner, you might use as your "telling 'em what you're going to tell 'em" statement, "Taking an inventory of one's life involves counting both physical and intangible substances. This morning I would like to discuss methods of taking such an inventory with the thought that we might end up with a greater skill in determining those things that can make us rich and, indeed, those things that can make us poor."

Why should you go through this exercise of being sure that the congregation knows in advance what you're going to say? Why not just save time and let them hear the various points as you make them? You need to prepare your listeners for what's coming. You've worked hard on planning and constructing each sermon point. You want your listeners to recognize them as major plateaus as you present them. Your listeners, in short, will be looking for these points if they are prepared to receive them. So you *should* "tell 'em what you're going to tell 'em."

Many homileticians firmly believe that the introduction is the most difficult part of the sermon to compose and the most challenging to deliver. Regardless of your appraisal of it—in terms of difficulty or importance—remember that a clear, well-honed introduction gives listeners a preview of the main sermon so they'll be able to recognize it when you run it past them.

5

How to Plan
the Main Body

Now that the warm-up exercises are complete, we move into the serious running: the body of the sermon, the fleshing out of the message you want to get across, the main reason you are in that pulpit. We're now at the second of the Perfect Preaching Principles—we "tell 'em." Let's review some basic fundamentals about this all-important section.

1. What is the object of your sermon?
2. What is the central thought running through it?
3. How is this central thought broken down into understandable units so they can be easily digested?

Cicero said there were five essentials in public speaking. As you read them, see how surprisingly relevant each is to the composition of the sermon's main body:

1. Determining exactly what one should say
2. Arranging the material in the proper order and with good judgment
3. Clothing the speech in well-chosen words and carefully phrased sentences
4. Fixing the speech in mind
5. Delivering it with dignity and grace

Get Facts Together

First, pull together all the facts you can collect about the subject. Here's where the recipe-box method comes in handy. I have such a box—it's about 10 inches long—containing 3-by-5 category tab cards covering a multitude of subjects. On these index cards are recorded topics I came upon at random (described in chapter 2). I also have my shoebox file into which I put all kinds of newspaper and magazine clippings, as well as bits and pieces of written memorabilia, particularly church bulletins, containing everything from meaty statements and current topic coverages to quotes and jokes—all potential material. Three other important sources should be consulted: the Bible, a good Bible commentary, and your own deep personal feelings, which moved you in the first place to pursue a given sermon topic. Examine them all very carefully.

Sometimes the human mind gets confused in trying to pull together an assortment of facts available for any subject. One of the most efficient ways to begin such a correlation and get at least a starting point is to take a lesson from Kipling, who, in referring to his "six honest serving-men," said:

> Their names are What and Why and When
> And How and Where and Who.

Kipling's verse may sound more like something the city editor would give to a cub reporter than a set of guidelines for compiling a good sermon. Remember, however, that if a sermon is written down in advance and Kipling's "serving-men" are kept in mind, chances are the sermon theme will be a complete one.

Divide the Sermon Into Sections

To avoid rambling, one-paragraph sermons, we need to divide the sermon into sections, which become "points." This assumes that the sermon subject is well chosen and deep enough to be divided in this way. If it's so shallow as to be covered in one section, you probably need another subject— or at least a new approach.

It's been properly argued that you can have a one-point sermon; that is, there's really only one point to be made. If the sermon is properly constructed, however, several divisions of reasoning will combine to produce the one major theme. These divisions of reasoning, therefore, automatically become separate points, or subpoints.

Every good sermon, therefore, must have at least two divisions, or points, and probably no more than three. Mind you, I've heard any number of four-point sermons and, on isolated occasions, five-point sermons. But in these instances, it took extreme skill both in the crafting of the message and, all impor-

tantly, in the delivery. For our purposes here, let's stick to the
two- or three-point body.

Exhaust Subject to Extract Points

You must now dissect your sermon subject so that it's perfectly clear. The logical way to see as many areas as possible
of the subject is to list all the relevant questions you can direct
to it. This may turn out to be a brainstorming checklist, lacking
in coherent order, but that's all right. This exhaustive search of
the topic will bring to the surface most of its shades and tones.

For instance, suppose a building addition to your sanctuary
has been proposed by the officers with the cost—pledge payments—to be spread over three years. The subject has caused
a division in the congregation. Several members, sensing potential damage to church unity, have suggested that you de-
vote a sermon to this situation. How do you tackle it?

First, get on with your random brainstorming list of questions directed at the question: To expand or not expand the
building. Here are some quick ones:

1. Why can't we keep on with our present building?
2. What needs will be served if we expand?
3. Can we afford the price tag?
4. Will it bring in more members?
5. Is there biblical encouragement to expand?
6. Will our yearly budget suffer because building gifts cut into
   regular pledges?
7. Should we not continue with the present crowded sanctuary,
   which indicates an "attractive" minister and quality of programs?
8. Suppose the economy collapses in the middle of construction and members can't pay off building pledges—what then?
9. Suppose the minister is called to another congregation during the first year of building. Will this discourage completion
   of pledge payments?
10. Suppose the character of the neighborhood changes, ad-
    versely affecting the value of our property. Won't we lose
    much?
11. Since the subject matter is new, why not think about it for
    another year and bring it up then?
12. If we expand and increase attendance and membership, we
    may need an assistant minister and extra staff. Are these
    added budget expenses too much on top of a building drive
    with delayed-payment pledges to be made?

13. Would our congregation assume a greater leadership role in the community because, with increased membership from building increase, we are larger?
14. Will the size of the organization required to handle such a campaign be a drain on our congregation and adversely affect other programs?
15. Can we afford increased property taxes, insurance, and maintenance?
16. Can the congregational divisions be resolved if we (a) have the addition or (b) don't have the addition?
17. How can we please both factions, regardless of final decisions?

With seventeen questions raised on this broad subject, to expand or not expand, we can group together those of a common thrust to get our sermon points. Three broad groupings appear as we skim through the questions: economic (E), Christian (C), and miscellaneous (M). Insert the proper code letter in front of each question.

You may argue that some of the codings apply to more than one question (number 16 might be either "M" or "C," since Christian unity and love are involved). No matter. This is a quick exercise designed to guide you in the direction of possible sermon points.

When we group together questions with the same coding, we get three divisions, each of which would be a sermon point. You, as minister, would announce that the sermon will discuss the proposed building addition from three viewpoints: economic indicators, miscellaneous considerations, and Christian reasoning. Here are the questions, grouped under these three points.

I. Economic Indicators

E 3. Can we afford the price tag?
E 6. Will our yearly budget suffer because building gifts cut into regular pledges?
E 8. Suppose the economy collapses in the middle of construction and members can't pay off building pledges— what then?
E 9. Suppose the minister is called to another congregation during the first year of building. Will this discourage completion of pledge payments?
E 10. Suppose the character of the neighborhood changes, adversely affecting the value of our property. Won't we lose much?

E 12. If we expand and increase attendance and membership,
      we may need an assistant minister and extra staff. Are
      these added budget expenses too much on top of a build-
      ing drive with delayed-payment pledges to be made?
E 15. Can we afford increased property taxes, insurance, and
      maintenance?

II. Miscellaneous Considerations

M 1. Why can't we keep on with our present building?
M 7. Should we not continue with the present crowded sanc-
      tuary, which indicates an "attractive" minister and qual-
      ity of programs?
M 11. Since the subject matter is new, why not think about it
      for another year and bring it up then?
M 13. Would our congregation assume a greater leadership
      role in the community because, with increased member-
      ship from building increase, we are larger?
M 14. Will the size of the organization required to handle such
      a campaign be a drain on our congregation and ad-
      versely affect other programs?
M 16. Can the congregational division be resolved if we (a)
      have the addition or (b) don't have the addition?
M 17. How can we please both factions, regardless of final
      decisions?

III. Christian Reasoning

C 2. What needs will be served if we expand?
C 4. Will it bring in more members?
C 5. Is there biblical encouragement to expand?

You will notice that the points regarding Christianity were
purposely placed last, because this spot is the normal place for
greatest emphasis. Assuming that you, the minister, are in
favor of such an expansion, your concluding thoughts can be
founded in an "O ye of little faith" mode. The sermon title
might be "When Is a Building Not a Building?" (obviously,
when it's a house of God).

The Thread of Coherence

Before getting into the mechanics of putting the body together, one word, "coherence," should be foremost. Coherence implies "thread." There must be the thread of a common

theme woven throughout the body. If a thread is literally suspended in midair, gravity will pull its loose end downward. Anything placed at the upward end of the thread, like a bead, will slide down it: again, pulled by gravity. If the thread running through a sermon body is visualized in this manner, every major and minor point structured into the message will automatically slide down the thread to the bottom—the sermon conclusion. This "thread" image will provide a forward movement to the sermon and keep it from becoming revolving, circular, or aimless.

One way to keep this thread intact from beginning to end is to keep the sermon title in mind—from beginning to end. I suggested in chapter 3 the practicality of placing two 3-by-5 cards (BEFORE and AFTER) in front of you while preparing the sermon to make certain the listener would leave the sanctuary a different—and better—person. If you have room on your desk, perhaps a third card with the title spelled out on it would draw your attention back to the subject and keep strong and straight the continuing discussion of *only* the subject.

Using Transitional Phrases

While the determination of these major sermon points in itself is a challenge, there's a fine tool available to help the flow of this order and actually to preach the order smoothly. This tool is the transitional phrase—just one or two words that lead you into the next major point. Some examples follow.

Then. The use of this word indicates that the discussion of one subject has ended and another subject is beginning. It separates two divisions: "He went to the closet and got out his coat; *then* he walked out the front door to his car." Sermonically speaking (as the first sermon point is concluded in a message about the duality of Jesus), "That explains why the humanity of Jesus was seen as his paramount characteristic by many in the multitudes. *Then,* let us remember"—this begins the second sermon point about Christ's divinity—"that his disciples saw him in a different light; they saw in him the divinity of God."

On the other hand. This phrase provides a natural twist to the closing of the first point and the introduction of the second point. Ending the first point we might find the statement, "This explains why tithing has proved to be such a difficult exercise for many Christians. *On the other hand,* we must look at what has happened to those who have taken this step and have seen the many blessings that can come from it." This contrasting device is a natural tool for switching to the next point.

Another way to approach this is . . . The use of this phrase causes the listener's mind to change gears and follow the preacher from the initial position to an alternative; the provision of a choice is often pleasing to the listener. An example might be: "So you can understand the frailty, the vacillation of humanity as expressed by Peter, for example, when he three times denied his Lord. But *another way to approach this* subject of humanity is to examine the strengths that can accrue to mere humans such as Paul and the other apostles, who risked life and limb for him after they recognized who the Master really was."

A variation of this phrase that makes it easy for the listener to move into the next point is *"and yet another reason why I take this position on this subject is that. . . ."* This phrase helps keep the listener's mind running along the theme thread and discourages it from wandering.

And on this subject of—————, we should not overlook . . . This phrase continues to hold on to the listener as if to imply, I'm not finished yet; keep listening. An example would be, "Aside from the two reasons I've already given you *on this subject of* choosing alternatives for living, *we should not overlook* a third choice, existing outside the scope of the first two, which is the fellowship of the church and God's grace."

Overview of the Skeleton

A good time to restate your sermon points comes as you move from one to another via the transitional phrase. Let's also put the body skeleton together. Assuming you're using a three-point sermon, the following format may be helpful:

1st Point	State point before beginning
	Finish
	Restate point
	Transitional phrase

2nd Point:	State point before beginning
	Finish
	Restate 1st and 2nd points
	Transitional phrase
3rd Point	State point before beginning
	Finish
Conclusion I	Restate all three points by "telling 'em what you told 'em"
Conclusion II	Cookie Cutter Close (see chapter 7)

This is not to say that all the above should be done in mechanical fashion. You must possess the flexibility to vary such a format without losing sight of its principal components and purpose.

To make certain the point is clear, and using again an oversimplification, here are some examples of moving from the second to the third point and finishing with the conclusion.

Not only is the practice of Christian charity beneficial to the recipient [1st sermon point] and helpful to the donor [2nd sermon point], now let's see how [transitional phrase] this practice of charity can benefit the church community [3rd point].

After you've finished the entire sermon body, you move through your two conclusions.

[*Conclusion I*] I hope that we can now agree that the practice of Christianity benefits all those who are involved in it directly and indirectly, because we've talked about how it affects the recipient, what it does for the donor, and, finally, how the church community is affected.
[*Conclusion II:* Cookie Cutter Close. This is a slowly drawn-out, deliberately spoken sentence or two that uses the theme of the sermon title as the very last words of your message. This close, which is the most important part of the sermon, is explained in chapter 7.]

Writing Out the Sermon

This business of writing down the sermon in advance simply raises another age-old argument about the effectiveness of advance writing for any kind of public speaking, preaching included.

About this art, Abbé Bautain, a nineteenth-century philosopher and theologian, said:

Writing is a whetstone which wonderfully stretches ideas. . . . If you have the time for preparation, never undertake to speak without having put on paper the sketch of what you have to say, the links of your ideas. You thus possess your subject better, and consequently speak more closely and with less risk of digressions. You understand it [the idea] better yourself, while spreading it out before your own eyes and unfolding it by words. . . . Experience teaches us that we are never fully conscious of all that is in our thoughts, except after having written it out. So long as it remains shut up in the mind it preserves a certain haziness. . . . Take pains to have the principal features well marked, vividly brought out, and strongly connected, in order that the . . . discourse may be clear and the links firmly welded.

Another way to look at Bautain's advice is to remember to have a plan and write it down. We have all heard sermons that seemed to have been given without much thought for their arrangement. These are what I call one-paragraph sermons, full of rambling thoughts, none of which seem to be connected with any coherence. The listener may be amazed by the outpouring of facts, encouragements, hopes, and scattered conclusions but will wonder at the end of the sermon what was said.

Another Frenchman, the Comte de Buffon, an eighteenth-century author and naturalist, said about writing what can also be said about preaching:

When he [the writer] has made a plan, when once he has brought together and put in order all the thoughts essential to his subject, he sees easily the instant when he ought to take up his pen, he will feel with certainty that his mind is ready to bring forth, he will be pressed to give birth to his ideas and will find only pleasure in writing; his ideas will succeed each other easily, and the style will be natural and ready; the warmth born of this pleasure will diffuse itself everywhere and give life to each expression; the animation will become higher and higher; the tone will become exalted; objects will take on color . . . the style will become interesting and luminous.

When you have a plan for your sermon, the elements seem to flow into place in logical order. It reminds me of watching a cook pour custard into a bowl: it spreads and settles by itself.

If you're still questioning the need to write out your sermon in advance, you might take some comfort from the fact that the eminent clergyman Harry Emerson Fosdick spent one hour in study for each minute of his sermon.

6

How to Construct
the Main Body

Now we move on from planning to the actual construction of the sermon body. Thus far, we've studied the introduction in some detail (chapter 4). After we review the construction of the sermon body, then, obviously, we will have to discuss the conclusion (chapter 7). As a review, let's put the purpose of these three units into perspective. First you attract attention to the subject through an introduction, which provides some sort of preview as to what's coming. Next, you break down the subject into orderly divisions, perhaps separated by a transitional phrase. Lastly, you wind up the sermon with a brief summary of what the sermon was basically about and what can be done with it.

Using normal sermon situations as a guide, we can see that a typical introduction can run anywhere up to a dozen sentences that take no more than one and a half minutes. At the other end, the conclusion will be less than twenty sentences —no more than two minutes. Obviously, the mass of the sermon is in its body.

Chronological Arrangement

There are any number of ways to arrange the sermon points. We are all probably most familiar with chronological order, in which a theme is developed in a series of what came first, second, etc. It's like the fairy tales we heard as children, which usually began, "Once upon a time." The tale started the listener at ground zero and then presented exactly what happened until, finally, the knight in shining armor—or whatever form the good guy took—emerged triumphant.

The following sample sermon outline is based on this arrangement. It involves David's wish to build God's temple, a task and a privilege that falls instead to Solomon. While I'll write out the introduction and the conclusion, I'm not going to spell out every word of the sermon. After you see the main points, you should be able to flesh out the body.

Sermon Title: Architect or Builder: Which Are You?
Scripture: 1 Chronicles 22:6–10 (New Testament
                 selection open)

Preface to the scripture reading: Our lesson selections will describe what was one man's dream and another man's accomplishment. We'll read how King David longed to build God's temple but wasn't selected because of his many acts of war. David's son Solomon was the man God chose for his temple builder, or, as we'd call such a person today, the general contractor. The name Solomon, incidentally, means man of peace.

Introduction: When we see a new building of any size constructed, there are usually two people behind it—the architect and the builder. On the one hand, the architect generally is a person of vision who sees not only what the final structure will look like but also knows what materials are required and what structural arrangement is needed for these materials. On the other hand, a builder often is a person who prefers to carry out plans already conceived.

Some of us are leaders, some are followers. Some of us are scientists while some are artists. Some of us are thick-skinned, some of us are overly sensitive. And some of us may be architects while some of us are builders.

Before this sermon is over, I hope we can all decide that we are both architect *and* builder insofar as the design and construction of a larger, more meaningful life for each of us is concerned as we exist within the framework of Christianity.

So much for the introduction. The three main divisions of this sermon that follow use the actual notes I would carry into the pulpit. You ought to be able to flesh out your own statements around these notes. You should also compose a transitional phrase between divisions (1) and (2), then another between divisions (2) and (3). Although this subject will be discussed at length in chapter 10, dealing with the style of the sermon, suffice it to say here that this method of using notes forces the preacher to break away, provides more opportunity for gestures, and allows more freedom of movement in the pulpit—all combining for a more personable, persuasive delivery.

The subject as outlined in the following notes is presented as an example only. It may be too simplistic and is certainly not particularly challenging. I've made my listing of notes—even the words—as clear as possible so that there'll be no misunderstanding about the format. An appropriate hymn for such a service would be "How Firm a Foundation."

1. PLAN FORMULATED (by you, the architect):
   A new life, a new building
   Human limitations (structural weaknesses)
   Human possibilities (structural strengths)
   Hero emulation
   Preacher (Peter Marshall)
   Missionary (Albert Schweitzer)
   Statesman (Gandhi)
   Humanitarian (Mother Teresa)
   Ultimate (Jesus Christ)

2. BUILDING STARTED (by you, the builder):
   Foundation laid (sand or rock)
   Materials available
   Family
   Prayer
   Church
   Gospel
   Quality of builder (self)
   Improving as construction proceeds

3. BUILDING COMPLETED
   How compares with original plans
   Would architect approve?
   Worthy of time spent?
   Glory to self?
   Glory to God?

Here is just one possible conclusion for this sermon theme. You'll notice that I use dots to indicate rather lengthy pauses between important phrases (see chapter 9). It's intended that the voice level drop considerably during the utterance of these words, but pay close attention to the spacing; this is most important. Remember, the most important part of a sermon is the last several sentences spoken:

Conclusion: There are few things in this life more tragic than a dreamer with a highly practical dream who can never see it come true. Moses had a dream—to enter the Promised Land—but God forbade this. David had a dream to build the temple, but it was denied this man of battle, as we read in our scripture lesson. But at least David turned out to be in large measure the architect not only of the building but of some of the rituals that were to take place in it.

As it turned out, the fortunate person was Solomon, who was the builder and saw come true this dream for a magnificent temple to God. So we see on the one hand an architect with a dream. We see, on the other hand, the builder carrying out the dream.

But you and I are in a somewhat different position. We can be both the architect *and* the builder. From this Sunday on, we can formulate our own plan by knowing our own limitations and calling upon our own strengths and, if necessary, using a great person of the past as our model. We can build our new building—our new life— using the materials readily available in our church and family lives. We can construct this edifice on the rock of the gospel rather than on the sand of humanity. And as we enter this construction program, using the plans we have so carefully formulated, we will find that the builder —ourselves—will increase in quality with each additional step of construction. And we will find that, if we follow these plans and have the necessary strengths, we will build a new building—a new temple—that will be to the glory of our new self and to the glory of God.

An architect or a builder—which are you? God . . . has given us . . . the architectural drawings [hold up small Bible]. He . . . has given us . . . the strengths . . . and building materials . . . required. It's . . . up to . . . you . . . and me. `
. . . . . . Let's . . . go . . . to work.

If you prefer a variation to the above conclusion, you might consider Oliver Wendell Holmes's "The Chambered Nautilus," which was quoted in chapter 2:

> Build thee more stately mansions, O my soul,
> As the swift seasons roll!
> Leave thy low-vaulted past!
> Let each new temple, nobler than the last,
> Shut thee from heaven with a dome more vast . . .

I didn't indicate pauses in Holmes's quote, but the last two lines should be drawn out extensively with a lowering of voice until the last words, "more vast," are completely isolated from their predecessors. Then wait at least five seconds before your invitation to prayer or the recital of the Apostles' Creed or whatever.

Problem–Solution Arrangement

Another sermon body format is the Problem-Solution. This type of order is almost self-explanatory, so I haven't gone into the detail of making notes for a sample sermon falling into this category, but I will give you a possibility for using this method. You realize, of course, that this involves the presentation of what could be called a problem—and you may be selecting an unusual problem involving the harmony of your congregation —and the subsequent solution associated with the problem. This, then, becomes a simple two-point sermon.

Let's select as the scripture Mark 10:17–22, the story of the rich man who asks Jesus about inheriting eternal life. You might choose as a sermon title "The Persistence of Priorities."

The introduction might include those perceptions required to recognize the important vs. the unimportant; the wheat vs. the chaff, the durable vs. the ephemeral, and so forth. In short, this ability to recognize—to categorize—vital areas of living can become (and usually does for Christians) a real problem. This will be your sermon message (you tell the congregation): that we all face these problems of decisions—particularly about the Christian use of money—and we plan to arrive at a solution to this problem before leaving the sanctuary.

The first sermon point in this two-point sermon would be the problem of recognizing and establishing priorities for life. This should be an easy point to develop, because so much emphasis is ordinarily placed on social and political prominence as well as on measuring a person in terms of physical possessions. The priority arrangement in which one places these possessions is, finally, the measurement of a person. The obvious question to be raised, therefore, is what priority, if any, does the person give to the love of God and eternal salvation vis-à-vis the love of money?

The second and final division of the sermon is the solution to one's reluctance to give high ranking to matters of the church. This was the case of the young man in the scriptures who wanted to hang on to his money because he was unwilling to place the proper priority on eternal life. The specific solution might be to present reasons substantial enough to be accepted by those who are open to such encouragements.

The conclusion can point out that we live unhappily and die unhappily when we, like the rich young ruler, lack the perception, courage, and strength to reorder our priorities. And one of the ironies of life is that you can be wealthy and unhappy at the same time—without proper priorities.

Contrast of Past and Present

From the title of this format, it is obvious that here is an opportunity to contrast what occurred in the past with what exists in the present. This approach can be used in connection with what used to be and what is proceeding now within the program of the church. The example I'll give here will be even skimpier than the ones given for the first two styles. A sermon title might be "The World's Oldest Campaign." The theme could be that the church was/is struggling for a stronger, clearer identity as a viable agent in the life of the world. For appropriate scriptures, the Old Testament is replete with instances involving attempts by heroes of the pre-Christian era to strengthen and hold together the early church. One thinks of Paul's writings for New Testament relevancies. While this may be a rather nebulous lead, the theme and thrust of the sermon could be what the church is trying to do and how the listener can help.

One danger about the past/present format is that you can get so caught up in the time span that the sermon could easily become too long. The art in this type of composition would be to use enough time to cover the past and present of a situation and also to make definitive urgings about what the listener can assume as personal goals for today's church. This reverts to an earlier point: "That was a fine sermon, but what does the minister expect me to do with it?"

Logical (Persuasive) Arrangement

This fourth main type of body format requires a little more creativity on your part, because you have to stop and think of what point logically comes first, second, and third. This style can be effectively used in making persuasive arguments. You must start your listeners at ground zero and then lead them forward through a logical progression to the final persuasive argument, which moves almost unnoticed into the conclusion.

A sample sermon title and selected scriptures on the subject of forgiveness, using this type of format, would be:

Sermon Title: Absolving Our Problems
Scriptures: Psalms 51:1–9
               Luke 23:32–34

Your introduction would indicate that this sermon will deal with some of the elements of the human psyche that seem continually to present problems for Christian living.

Since the subject of the sermon is forgiveness, the sermon body would have to start at the first logical point, which is to examine those characteristics that interfere with the exercise of forgiveness. To preserve logical coherence, you might start with our natural human reluctance to forgive and our tendency to seek retribution. You can mention other failings that seem to be natural extensions of these unfortunate characteristics, many of which lead into feelings of inadequacy. (Martin Luther had frequent bouts of depression because of low self-esteem.)

A conclusion could be based upon (in logical order) the need to understand the individual's worth in God's sight, which leads to a renewed self-appraisal; a new look at the worth of others because of our understanding of our value in God's sight; then (again in logical order) the renewed strength we can find through these conclusions to forgive others. Only then, after having asked God to "absolve our problems," can we honestly pray that portion of the Lord's Prayer, "Forgive us our debts, as we forgive our debtors."

While you will no doubt want to choose your own sermon topics, the use of a logical order to persuade is vital, regardless of the subject matter. In writing business letters, for instance, I've frequently used what I call a freewheeling method of persuasion by starting off something like this (from a letter I was asked to write encouraging business leaders to give summer employment to youths):

You may have seen recent press notices concerning the need for responsible businesses in our community to make every effort to hire teenagers during the summer months. This, as you surely know, gives them valuable experience for their later business endeavors and eliminates a lot of idle time which might be potentially dangerous.

The truth of the matter is that the reader may or may not have seen the press notice and may or may not know about the salutary effects of teenage employment. But at least this approach provides a starting point (the newspaper article) for absorbing my arguments.

7

How to Construct the Conclusion

We have come to the last Perfect Preaching Principle: We tell 'em what we told 'em. As I have said, this part of the sermon—the conclusion—is the most important.

A bit of creativity is required to vary the way you begin your conclusions from week to week. If you experience difficulty in summarizing in this manner, it may be because the thread of the sermon theme is not coherent (see chapter 5). You may have to revise your main points.

Fortunately, however, there can at least be a similarity among these possibilities for concluding. You can start on the note, "So that's what we've been reviewing this morning—the need to . . . [spell out your sermon points]." Using as an example the sample sermon in chapter 6, you might say, "As we pull together our thinking on building that sanctuary addition, we need to take a good look at the economic factors involved—those that face us now and what could turn up down the road—as well as the pros and cons of moving ahead as we try to interpret our Christian responsibility. Can we do it? Should we chance it?"

It is important to get back to the sermon title, either the actual title or a slight paraphrase of it, to truly establish the thread of coherency from the beginning of the introduction to this part of the conclusion. *Then* you go into the final concluding statements, examples of which follow.

The Sermon's Focal Point

The last several sentences of a sermon, while they are certainly a part of the conclusion, are really a matter of emphasis. And the degree—the strength—of any emphasis relies primarily on its position. Marketing people will tell you that the outside of the back cover of a magazine is the best place to advertise—and the most expensive. Operating on the Theory of Primacy and Recency (as mentioned in chapter 4), you must make your most important point last. As in back-cover advertising, the wares of a sermon are best displayed at the end. This is especially true—as I've said before—if these several sentences are drawn out slowly, with almost painful deliberation, thereby making certain that the congregation thoroughly understands the meat of the sermon through this method of summarizing.

When you hear a twenty-minute sermon, the words you will probably remember above all others are the last ones—particularly if they are spoken slowly, carefully, and deliberately so that they can be savored by both the speaker and the listener. To repeat: This is the crucial part of the sermon.

The Cookie Cutter Close

This sort of conclusion is what I call a Cookie Cutter Close. If you've ever watched someone cut out cookies, you'll notice that the cookie cutter is pressed deliberately and firmly onto the rolled-out dough to punch or stamp out each cookie. Similarly, the utterance of the words in the last several sentences of your conclusion should be measured and drawn out—with a somewhat lowered voice—to the point where you are carefully stamping them out as if with a cookie cutter. If you think this sounds silly, imagine trying to punch out a series of cookies as rapidly as some preachers seem to want to get rid of the last several sentences of their sermon. The best rate of speed you can achieve with a cookie cutter is about one cookie every two seconds. You may think this pace is too slow for speaking, but if you're measuring out these words—and there are not really that many words in the last several sentences—you can easily see how they can be stamped out for individuality and proper emphasis, to be savored—and remembered.

Let's look at it another way. You're committing an unwitting crime against the time, talent, and training that go into the preparation and presentation of your sermon if you don't learn to wrap it up properly in these last few seconds. You may spend hours or days in selecting, fashioning, and polishing your sermon; not to be able to close it with words that will be remembered is to defeat your purpose and your work.

The Wrap-Up

Here's an example. Your wedding anniversary is coming up. You head for the nearest department store and spend about an hour walking up and down the aisles trying to spot an appropriate gift. No luck. You go to the department store at the other end of the shopping mall and do the same. No luck. You go in a specialty shop, sure that if you couldn't find the proper gift in the first two stores, you'll certainly find it here. You do. It turns out to be the blow dryer you see pictured on a point-of-purchase sign on the counter beside the cash register. You tell the clerk, "That's what I want." The clerk disappears into the stockroom in the back and comes out carrying the usual brown, utilitarian-looking box with the manufacturer's name and the product serial number emblazoned on several sides: not a very attractive container. You breathe a sigh of relief, however, because several hours of search finally prove to be successful. The clerk takes your money, puts the box in a bag, gives you your receipt and change, and off you go triumphantly.

On the morning of the anniversary, you get out the bag before breakfast, hand it to your spouse, and offer the expected salutation, "Happy anniversary, dear." Your spouse unfolds the rumpled bag, reaches inside, extracts the blow dryer in its plain commercial box, and exclaims over the gift. "Honey, this is just what I wanted."

Your spouse, out of basic goodness, patience with you, and delight at receiving the gift wouldn't think of indicating that, while your present would be appreciated in any state, it would have meant more if it had been gift-wrapped. What if the brown box had been covered with beautiful paper and encircled by a colored ribbon with a bow? What a difference between the two presentations!

Like a marriage partner, congregations are patient. They are pleased to receive what they consider a reasonably good sermon. But how much more wonderful a gift the sermon would be with all the wrappings. The congregation, too, would be carried to an even higher level of enjoyment with a complete presentation and final wrap-up.

The same thing applies in the searching, selecting, and wrapping up of your Sunday "gift"—your sermon. You can spend hours looking for a subject and an interesting title, you can agonize in researching, consulting notes, praying, and pulling out all the stops to organize your message for the next Sunday, which is always just around the corner. But to do all this work and then bring your sermon to the point of presentation without a deliberate Cookie Cutter Close is the cruelest of fates, both for your sermon, which undoubtedly deserves better treatment, and certainly for your congregation. The substance (the blow dryer) is there, but is it properly wrapped up?

Remember that, like the jogger, you need stretching exercises before tearing around the block (see chapter 3). Similarly, like the jogger who winds down slowly to let the muscles cool off, you will need to wind your sermon down slowly, deliberately, and with measured spacing.

If you remember nothing from this book except one sentence, please remember this one: The most important thing a preacher says from the pulpit on Sunday morning is the last several sentences of the sermon: the Cookie Cutter Close.

Here are some Cookie Cutter Closes for a couple of sermon subjects. In each case remember that your summary conclusion statement—the "tell 'em what you told 'em" summary—should have just been made at this point.

Example 1. On one occasion when I was asked to give a sermon on the subject of the stewardship of time, I chose for a scripture Matthew 25:41–46 ("I was hungry but you did not feed me"), etc. My sermon title was "Equivalent Concern," and I summarized it by closing with a review of what would happen on Judgment Day when we would all be held accountable for the treatment we had given our fellow humans in varying circumstances. The conclusion went something like this:

> Because of my inaction in this area of helping others, I certainly don't look forward to the Judgment Day pictured in our scripture lesson. I'm afraid that the King on his throne will lean forward and look at me and say, "Hank, when I was hungry, why didn't you give me something to eat? When I needed clothing, why didn't you share something from your bulging wardrobe? When I was in the hospital, where were you? When I was in prison and would have longed for your company, if only for a few moments, what happened to you and to this equivalent concern you expressed for me and your fellow humans?"

Here are the last sentences of my Cookie Cutter Close.
Three dots equal one second:

When . . . he . . . looks at me . . . with that question,
. . . what . . . am I . . . going . . . to say? . . . [Here the voice
is raised, as if crying out for assistance in this dilemma.]
What . . . *am I . . . going . . . to say!* [This sentence is spoken
in almost a state of dejected hopelessness, measured out
with lowered voice but still audible in the back pew.] What
. . . am I . . . going . . . to say?

Now comes the *most crucial* sentence in the entire sermon. I
waited a full five or six seconds for that last question to sink
in before I seemed to get new life and asked:

"What . . . . . . are *you* . . . . . . going . . . . . . to say?"

I got several calls at home that afternoon, one of which I shall
never forget. The dear lady called me and said that she had not
noticed a close friend in the congregation, so she called her on
the telephone to say what a marvelous sermon she had missed.
The friend responded that she had heard the sermon on the
radio and certainly did think it was fine. But—and this is the
main point—the woman who called me said that she told her
friend, "That's all well and good, but you should have been
there to actually see how he stood there, without moving, to
let his last words sink in."

Example 2. Here's a closing I used another time when
asked to give a sermon when our church was without a minister. As in the case of most churches—especially downtown
churches—some groups within the congregation had slightly
different concepts of conducting the business of the church,
especially in this interim period. I chose as my title "Boundaries of Patience." My texts were Exodus 32:7–10 and Matthew 21:12–13. The sermon went back in history and included several examples of what could happen when schisms
developed in governments, particularly in the early church, and
how these potential disruptions and divisions could occur
within our congregation—if we were not careful. My appeal
was to reexamine the boundaries of our individual patience
with the thought that they could be strengthened as we tried
to keep the interests and needs of our congregation foremost
in our minds during this period. My conclusion was something
like this:

We have reviewed this morning the upheavals within government and church caused by certain individuals who reached the boundaries of their patience. We have seen that, without this important human quality, disruption— and, indeed, chaos—can easily come about.

And here was my last line.

For the sake of this congregation and for everything that it has done in the past and can do in the future, let us . . . reexamine our own . . . boundaries . . . of . . . patience . . . and call upon God . . . for him to share . . . an even greater portion of his patience with us . . . so that . . . this congregation . . . can be strengthened . . . and preserved . . . to get on . . . . . . with the work . . . . . . of the kingdom . . . . . . in this place . . . . . . at . . . this . . . . . . time.

Example 3. Another stewardship sermon possibility might bear the title "Felt Hilarious Lately?" The sermon could be based on the passage "God loves a cheerful giver" but would explain that the Greek root for "cheerful" is really "hilarious." The sermon could contain examples of gifts freely given by yourself or known to have been given by others. In such cases, the assurance of having complied with God's requests regarding liberality can not only bring about a powerful good to the recipient (including the church) but also provide incredible happiness (hilarity) to the donor.

As you get closer to the end of the last sentence, insert more spaces—in Cookie Cutter style—before the final several words. (To measure seconds you can count slowly, under your breath: "One second, two seconds," and so on.)

When you use generous liberality in those instances when you clearly see the needs of others and the church, you are in one of the few situations where you can really . . . know . . . what the . . . scripture writer . . . tried to tell you . . . . . . that you . . . can be indescribably . . . happy because . . . you have become a recipient . . . of God's thanks . . . and you know this . . . because . . . God . . . loveth . . . a hilarious . . . . . . giver. . . . . . . Have *you* . . . felt . . . . hilarious . . . . lately?

You will notice that the word "hilarious" has more of a pause on each side of it than any other word in the conclusion. Why? because this word is the *key* word—in the sermon title and in the body. It's the *last* thought the congregation should remember as they leave the sanctuary. Read it again.

Example 4. For another sermon title you might use "Aristocrats I Have Known." This potential message is based on the subject of gratitude. No specific scripture background is suggested here—the Bible is full of such themes—but I have in mind the secular axiom, "Gratitude is the aristocrat of emotions."

The sermon body might confront the sin of ingratitude and what ills such a hardness produces: greed, petulance, paranoia, inability to break out into the joyfulness of life. These unfortunate qualities are presented in their weak positions vs. the rich (aristocratic) living of a grateful person.

For examples of the aristocrats of the sermon title, you might select secular heroes who have made sacrifices out of their gratitude, followed by biblical characters who demonstrated this same trait.

I would end such a sermon like this:

> We would all do well to leave this place grateful for our forebears who created this very place—this country, this church—where we are at this moment; grateful for friends who tolerate our weaknesses; grateful for families that give us a unit of incomparable strength; grateful for the church that provides us with this sacred home. Let us be, therefore . . . the aristocrats we all can be . . . through the exercise of an acute sense of gratitude . . . which can help us . . . be better persons for ourselves to enjoy . . . better persons for others to enjoy . . . and better . . . and stronger . . . . . . people . . . . . . in the service . . . . . . of the greatest Aristocrat . . . . . . of all . . . . even Jesus Christ our Lord.

The greatest fault of many preachers I've heard over the years is their failure to get back to their sermon title (which, after all, is the subject) in the last words of their sermon. Their title inevitably is developed to a point but then dropped, as the sermon ends on a subject—not the title—that seems to have evolved along the way.

So get back to the title, if only through a paraphrase, but mention it—spell it out—either in your summary or in the Cookie Cutter Close.

Always assuming there's some degree of coherence

throughout your introduction and body, getting back to the title will indicate a direct, consistent line of thought all the way from the beginning to the very end. See the four examples above.

How about the common practice of saying "Amen" immediately following the last words of the sermon conclusion? Ministers may do this because (1) they feel that traditionally it's the only proper thing to do, (2) they find it difficult to come up with an alternative, or (3) the congregation expects them to do it. However, I don't recommend using "Amen" at that point.

If the Cookie Cutter Close is used as described—that is, if you've spoken slowly, painstakingly, and deliberately—the word "Amen" produces a puncturelike sound that dilutes the emotion of these last words. It's like pricking a balloon with a pin: One minute the balloon—the conclusion—is there, the next minute it isn't. To put it another way, the word "Amen" at this point comes like a rifle shot to startle listeners out of the reflective quietude they should be in during the final words of the sermon. I would much rather see the minister stand there for six or seven seconds without moving a muscle, waiting for the last drawn-out words of the conclusion to sink in.

There are several options for ending the sermon *after* you've waited these six or seven seconds without saying "Amen," depending, of course, upon your usual order of worship. For instance, if your congregation normally recites the Apostles' Creed, you could take one step backward, raise your arms upward, and say, "May we stand and recite together the Apostles' Creed." Or you might simply say, "Let us pray," providing thanks for the word of God which was the foundation for the sermon and an appeal for strength to carry out the possibilities for service the message may have covered.

Other order-of-worship items that follow the sermon, such as the offering and pastoral prayer and even a closing hymn, should confirm and not detract from your theme. There is a chance, however, that these other elements may dilute your last sermon words. These last sermon words, therefore, must be so carefully chosen—and so deliberately and slowly delivered—that their effect will survive and be remembered after the close of the service.

I've heard some outstanding sermons that got started with an attention-getting opening sentence. But good introduction or not, good sermon body or not, without a strong, deliberate close, the sermon experience is sometimes difficult for people to retain—after they walk out the door. So close it up, wrap it up, and stretch it out—for the sake of impression and retention.

8

Reducing the Sermon to Notes

Let's go to the actual notes you take with you into the pulpit when following the extemporaneous form of preaching. The sample sermon "Easy Come, Easy Go," which follows shortly, is purposely quite simple in content in order to illustrate the actual sermon words to be spoken vs. the notes you will use as cues for the spoken words themselves.

You will see that there are two levels of notes. The first, step 1, is a rather full set and may be the kind you prefer to use first. It's like putting a toe in the water before you jump in. The briefer "graduate-level" notes (the kind you'll eventually get to use) appear in step 2.

Refer first to the right-hand column in step 1 under Spoken Statements to see the actual message composition. It's best to ignore the left-hand column, Pulpit Notes, until you've read the seven paragraphs on the right, spelling out the words of the sermon body, several times. Writing out the entire sermon in this fashion permits easy revision before the entire sermon body is wrapped up.

Now, assuming you've read the paragraphs on the right often enough to be reasonably familiar with them, you should read the pulpit notes on the left to see how the cues are recorded. It may be that the cues you'll choose will be somewhat different. Use whatever notes you feel comfortable with.

Next, cover up the right-hand side of the page, the spoken statements, and try to say these same statements out loud using only the pulpit notes on the left. You may have to sneak a peek to tie the note with the statement. But eventually, experience will allow you to take only the brief notes on the left into the pulpit. The selection of the notes themselves will become

Step 1 (elementary)

Easy Come, Easy Go

Pulpit Notes	*Spoken Statements*
If tempted to quit (try new life) think of sacrifices become Christian.	If you've ever been tempted to give up your Christian beliefs and try an easier brand of new living, think for a minute about what steps you took, and what sacrifices you may have made, to become a Christian.
May be lifetime regular member. May be recently joined just starting to enjoy new blessing.	You may have been brought up in the church and been a regular church school attender most of your life. Or you may have recently joined this church and are just beginning to experience the blessings of Christianity.
Regardless of strength of membership, would give up something. If ties are strong, would give much. If ties weak, not much (Easy Come, Easy Go).	In any event, no matter how firm or loose your affiliation is, you would have to give up something if you decided to leave Christian living. If your belief—your membership, your affiliation, your dedication—is strong, the act is more severe and the loss is greater. If your relationship is weak and is hardly a secondary part of your life, then parting is less painful and may be considered as Easy Come, Easy Go.
Assume we have strong ties. Most of us always here (this shows interest). If inventory what we would lose Better appreciate what all would have Stick it out— Stand by	Let's assume most of our ties are strong (most of us are here every Sunday and our attendance, at least, indicates more than just casual interest). This way, by taking an inventory of what we would lose by quitting the church (and unfortunately many people are), we will be able to better appreciate what we will continue to have when we stick it out and stand by—and live—those principles of our church.

Step 1
(Continued)

Pulpit Notes	Spoken Statements
Heard of addict's testimony rehabilitation funds. Committee thought wasted. Asked addict what prevented return. Hell I was in not worth going back.	I once heard on the news a recovered drug addict testifying before a government body regarding the need of more funds for rehabilitation. A committee member said he thought it was wasted money. He asked the former addict, "Can't you revert to this habit any time? What keeps you from giving up your freedom from drugs and going back to the habit?" The former addict responded, "All I have to do is think about the hell I was in, and I decide it's not worth going back."
To give up new Christian "highs" Not much different from addict's return To unguided, uncharted slavery to former undisciplined master.	Giving up the freedom—the euphoria —the "highs" of a true Christian life (often a new-found freedom), is not very different from the addict who is reluctant to take up again the vividly recalled, unguided, uncharted, demonic slavery of the flesh to a stronger master.
Should inventory stock we'd give up (assets for living/dying) Which would be ours if hold fast.	So now we should inventory those areas we would give up by casting off our Christian ties, and count as assets for living—and dying—those features which would be ours if we hold fast.

more important as you learn to choose those words which best represent the statements they stand for.

You'll notice that at this level of note taking, not too many words have been omitted from the spoken statements in selecting their corresponding pulpit notes. Such reasonably full notes almost spell out the statements. If you feel the need to do so, you can, of course, make these pulpit notes even more complete so that they even more fully resemble the entire spoken statement. The beautiful part about this type of note taking is that they can be accordionized to match both your willingness to extemporize and your experience in this type of preaching. The less experience you have, the more complete the notes should be. The greater your experience in this method—and the growing confidence that will accrue as your experience expands—the fewer notes you will need.

Now let's try the graduate level, with fewer pulpit notes. This assumes that you are familiar enough with the sermon to use them.

Step 2 (advanced)

Easy Come, Easy Go

Pulpit Notes	*Spoken Statements*
Before quit think sacrifice	If you've ever been tempted to give up your Christian beliefs and try an easier brand of living, think for a minute about what steps you took, and what sacrifices you may have made, to become a Christian.
Lifetime member Recent convert	You may have been brought up in the church and been a regular church school attender most of your life. Or you may have recently joined this church and are just beginning to experience the blessings of Christianity.
If leave—sacrifice something Strong ties— Parting hard Weak ties Easy come, go	In any event, no matter how firm or loose your affiliation is, you would have to give up something if you decided to leave Christian living. If your belief—your membership, your affiliation, your dedication—is strong, the act is more severe and the loss is greater. If your relationship is weak and is hardly a secondary part of your life, then parting is less painful and may be considered as Easy Come, Easy Go.
Assume strong ties (most always here) Inventory losses Appreciate will have when stand by	Let's assume most of our ties are strong (most of us are here every Sunday and our attendance, at least, indicates more than just casual interest).

Step 2
(Continued)

Pulpit Notes	*Spoken Statements*
	This way, by taking an inventory of what we would lose by quitting the church (and unfortunately many people are), we will be able to better appreciate what we will continue to have when we stick it out and stand by—and live—those principles of our church.
Addict—hearing Committee questioned cure permanence Hell not worth it	I once heard on the news a recovered drug addict testifying before a government body regarding the need of more funds for rehabilitation. A committee member said he thought it was wasted money. He asked the former addict, "Can't you revert to this habit any time? What keeps you from giving up your freedom from drugs and going back to the habit?" The former addict responded, "All I have to do is think about the hell I was in, and I decide it's not worth going back."
Sacrifice "highs" Reluctant reassume slavery	Giving up the freedom—the euphoria—the "highs" of a true Christian life (often a new-found freedom), is not very different from the addict who is reluctant to take up again the vividly recalled, unguided, uncharted, demonic slavery of the flesh to a stronger master.
Let's inventory retained blessings When hold fast	So now we should inventory those areas we would give up by casting off our Christian ties, and count as assets for living—and dying—those features which would be ours if we hold fast.

Now that you are totally familiar with the sermon (methods of practicing it will be developed later), you are in a position to carry into the pulpit just enough sheets of note paper (about 5 by 8 inches is the right size to fit into a hymnbook or personal Bible) in sufficient quantity to hold your outline of pulpit notes. This is also a good size on which to record special announcements and provide cues about elements in the order of worship.

The Skill of Quick-Glancing

Now comes the skill—and it's easily acquired—that comes from the practice of quick-glancing at groups of words. These groups of words are to be found as two possibilities in your notes. They are the words that comprise either one line or the several lines which, together, provide the group cue.

For instance, if you look back at the pulpit notes in step 2 (and let's concentrate on this step instead of the more elementary step 1), you will see that the first cue (group 1) is made up of two lines:

Before quit
   think sacrifices

Here's an entire thought expressed in just four words extracted from the first seven lines shown under Spoken Statements. If you practice the phrase "Before quit, think sacrifices," your spoken statement could come out in a variety of ways—as long as you understand what these four cue words mean.

For instance, you might start out by saying, "If you've ever thought about getting away from some of the Christian practices you've been following, you may want to think about the changes you had to make—and the things you had to give up —in order to become a Christian."

Or you might say something like, "I suppose all of us, at one time or another, have thought about how much easier it would be to throw away the rigorous type of life we sometimes seem to have as Christians and just give it up for an easier brand of living—without even thinking about some of the drastic changes and things we sacrificed to call ourselves practicing Christians." The fact that there are slight differences between these two statements is unimportant. They both mean essentially the same thing, because they both come from the thoughts expressed in the two-line cue.

These two examples are even somewhat different from the actual words under Spoken Statements, but *all three* are saying the same thing.

Easy Come, Easy Go

Before quit think sacrifices	Group 1
Lifetime member Recent convert	Group 2
If leave sacrifice something	Group 3
Strong ties Parting hard	Group 4
Weak ties Easy come, go	Group 5
Assume strong ties most always here	Group 6
Inventory losses	Group 7
Appreciate will have when stand by	Group 8

Separating Sub-Thoughts

Our next group of statements (group 2) is made up of two "sub-thoughts" comprising one larger group of thoughts. You will notice that this group of two thoughts is separated from the first group by a wider space. At a quick glance while preaching, this important space tells you that you are shifting gears to another point. To make sure that these two sub-thoughts don't become connected to the preceding group (1) of two lines and the third group (3), which is next, these two sub-thoughts are separated from each other by only a slight space. If need be, just for this study, you can draw a circle around each group of two sub-thoughts to make them hang together.

Familiarity Permits Flexibility

No matter how often you review your pulpit notes in practicing the sermon, chances are the spoken statements will never quite be the same in each practice session. This doesn't mean that you shouldn't try to hone these statements so that they will come out exactly as you want them to. This takes additional practice, experience, and skill. But if you feel strongly enough about your points and you understand them well enough, the essence of what you want to say will be there, available to you, in this type of note taking.

The best way to use this method of abbreviated notes is to keep your forefinger sliding down the page of notes as each point is made. This allows you to look up at your congregation most of the time. Your necessary glances down at the notes will require less time than you think if you have mastered the art of grasping the entire sentence meaning from the thought groups—regardless of exactly how the sentence words come out. Also, by keeping your left forefinger on the notes, you can easily take one step to your right, for example, and let it be joined by your left foot while, at the same time, keeping your left forefinger directly under the note under discussion. This simple one-step movement breathes an unbelievable amount of life into the sermon presentation (see chapter 13). It removes the illusion that the preacher's feet are glued in two spots directly behind the pulpit.

You can of course reverse this procedure by putting your right forefinger under the set of notes under discussion and move one step to the left. If you only do this twice during the entire sermon (once to the right and once to the left), you'd be amazed at the effect of this movement from the parishioners' side of the pulpit. It indicates that you are more relaxed than you actually may be. It also suggests that you have complete control over the sermon, since you are at liberty to move around.

Obviously, this act of keeping your forefinger on your notes while moving to one side or the other can be rather awkward if not done smoothly. You shouldn't have to resort to this procedure too long; even slight experience with this method will gradually eliminate the need to use it indefinitely. In other words, consider it a training tool.

9

Lord, How Do You Want Me to Read That Line?

Let's turn now to the actual speaking of the words, rather than how they are composed. But first, a little background.

Those of you who are avid readers of syndicated columns have learned to pick and choose among certain writers whose work you enjoy reading. Or you may have reached the point where you frequently skip a particular author's column because you can tell by the headline exactly what he or she will say—and you're not interested in the subject. Such has become the case with me.

In my picking and choosing, I almost bypassed a column by Andy Rooney in mid-August, 1982, until a second look indicated that this was one I should read. It was entitled "A Talented, Hard-Working Professional Actor," and there was a line drawing of the late actor Henry Fonda in the middle of the column. The article was written shortly after Mr. Fonda's death. It involved Rooney's one-character Broadway play about Franklin Delano Roosevelt. Henry Fonda had been selected to take the part.

The startling lines for me came where Mr. Rooney was describing the initial reading of his script.

> I was sitting to the side and Fonda stopped and turned toward me. (He knew my name now.)
> "How do you want me to read that, Andy? Do you want it like that or like this?"
> He read it again, changing the rhythm and the emphasis of his voice to give it another nuance of meaning.

Here was a great actor, skilled in orally interpreting the writings of others. Even with his vast experience, he deferred to the author to make certain he was giving the proper meaning and expression to the writer's words. A preacher in the pulpit on Sunday morning, or officiating at a funeral service or a wedding—or on any other occasion involving the reading of scripture—is doing nothing less than Henry Fonda in that he or she is reading words written by another person. Andy Rooney wrote a story of Franklin Delano Roosevelt. Scripture writers wrote a story of creation, the matter of women and men, a story of redemption and salvation—a story of eternal life. Which "author" (Rooney vs. David the psalmist, for example) shall we read in which way—or shall they both be read the same way? Or shall we turn to the author and ask how he wants the lines read? In the case of Henry Fonda, the author was sitting onstage. In your case, the author is unavailable for questioning, which puts the burden of interpretation directly on you.

Getting at the Meat of the Words

After selecting the scripture for the sermon, the careful expositor examines the context in which the passage was written and comes to some conclusion about the frame of mind of the author. Was he angry or sad (in which case you don't want to read his words with a broad grin or a beaming face)? Or was he joyous and full of good news (now the smile, not the scowl)? In a few pages, we'll talk about scrutinizing each word with the understanding that certain words need emphasis; with this emphasis, the words, the verse, and the whole scripture lesson almost take on a different meaning.

A couple of my preacher friends reacted with mild shock at the idea of reading scripture the way the author may have wished it read. To them, anything that smacks of play-acting is repulsive and outside the realm of the Holy Spirit's role in sermonic efforts. I asked one of these friends, "Well, then, how do you prepare yourself to read the scripture lesson during your morning worship service?"

He said, "I ask that the Holy Spirit be with me during my readings and my sermon—and in fact, throughout the entire service—and use me as he sees fit. This way, I know that he just wants me to be myself, so I make no other effort beyond that."

I then asked, "Why did you go to the seminary?"

He looked at me in surprise. "Is that a serious question, not a rhetorical one?"

I replied that it was indeed a serious question.

He answered, "I went to the seminary to learn those things that I could only learn at a seminary. I learned how to become a preacher, how to become a minister—to take care of a flock —and how to become, to the best of my ability, a man of God and a servant of Jesus Christ."

I pointed out that there are many new learning experiences to which those entering a seminary are exposed for the first time, not the least of which is the need to increase one's skill in the field of oral interpretation. And one giant step forward in this process is to imagine that you have the opportunity to ask the author of any given verse Henry Fonda's question: "How do you want me to read that line?" Without this exercise, your readings will remain at a level far less than your ministry and your witness to Jesus Christ deserve.

Asking the Author

By way of a start let's raise the question, "Paul, how do you want me to read your letter to the Corinthians?"

Paul was apparently feisty on certain occasions, and this personality trait must be considered when we read some of his letters. For instance, we see in some of them a degree of impatience with certain of his churches. He might tell us, if such a conversation were possible, that he wrote a certain letter with very strong feelings, and we would be remiss if we read that letter in a phlegmatic, weak, and unfeeling tone. He might even go so far as to say, "I certainly hope you bang on that pulpit a couple of times, because that is exactly what I felt like doing when these brethren disregarded some of the things I asked them to do." You should feel that Paul is depending upon you to read his lines in the spirit in which he wrote them.

But now, to get down to the speaking of the words themselves, let's take a look at the Twenty-third Psalm. Except for the Lord's Prayer, this is probably the most loved and best known scripture, which accounts for the fact that, simply because of its familiarity, it's often spoken by rote.

It is really disturbing to hear this psalm read at a funeral in an awkward, singsong manner. This happened recently at a service for a fairly young man who died of leukemia. My heart went out to his wife and daughters. The minister said, "Let us .urn to the scriptures for words of comfort at this time of loss," and he read, totally mechanically and with no feeling whatsoever, "The Lord is my shepherd; I shall not want. He maketh me to lie down in green pastures," etc., etc. If he really wanted to provide comfort, the minister would have raised the question in advance: "David, how do you want me to read these lines?" For these lines *are* a source of comfort.

The minister could also have asked himself, "Why did David write this in the first place, and why is this psalm so popular that it's better remembered over and above much of holy writ? Why is it considered a study in confidence, a source of strength and comfort in time of woe? How would David have us say them?"

Let's take a good look at the author. Why did David write this psalm, and what were his feelings when he wrote it? If you were in my class, I would draw out of you the various emotions that David may have felt and list the answers on the blackboard. Among some of the possible feelings you might suggest (contentment, gratitude, security, pride), I would jump quickly on the suggestion of pride, although you might select gratitude as David's prime motivation for this writing.

David seems to be telling us that he was proud of having chosen God to be his shepherd rather than any number of kings who reigned at the time, any number of spirits, or any number of false gods. It's refreshing to note that a shepherd has admitted that he himself needs a shepherd. But whom did he choose? He chose the Lord God—the Mighty Father. David is saying, in effect, "I don't know whom you chose for your shepherd, but I want you to listen very carefully about the one I chose. I want to tell you about him, what he has done for me and what he will continue to do for me." He gives us, then, not just a weak, delicate, pretty poem that might cause us to dab at our eyes with a handkerchief, but a vigorous, thrusting description of the power of his mighty but at the same time loving shepherd.

Starting the Emphasis Exercise

Let's see if we can get David's real intent out of his first line. Boldfaced words that are underlined indicate a strong point of emphasis, at which time the voice is heavier and more assertive. Boldfaced words that are not underlined simply mean a mild degree of emphasis—but certainly stronger than no emphasis at all. As in chapter 7, three dots equal one second.

David, how do you want me to read this line?

The **Lord** . . . . . . is **my** . . . shepherd.

David seems to rear up to his full height and say, "Choose whom you may for your shepherd, but I've chosen the Lord God Almighty." Pay special attention to the spacing. And remember that the underline under the boldfaced word "Lord" shows that you can almost shout it out to indicate this pride. Practice raising your voice when you reach this word. The word "my" can be given a milder shout, but it still needs some emphasis.

The second line of this psalm should be said in a firm, steadily paced measure, with particular separate emphasis on each word (note the spacing, but also note that each word has the same emphasis), leaving no room for equivocation:

I . . . shall . . . not . . . want.

To round off this firm statement, you might place an exclamation point at the end of the sentence, in your mind.

If you read this the way you think David wants you to, you tie these two lines together and repeat firmly, and with no small degree of pride, his announcement to all ages about this person whom he has chosen to be his shepherd and his statement (in the second line) of what will happen to him as a result of his selection. Let's put them together.

The **Lord** . . . . . . is **my** . . . shepherd,
I . . . shall . . . not . . . want.

Now we get into an interesting area, because David seems to feel the need to elaborate further on why he has selected the Lord as his shepherd. In the verses that follow, he starts listing, in menu style, the reasons for his choice to make absolutely certain that we understand. You might imagine that at this point David is holding up one hand, with his fingers spread apart, and is using the forefinger of the other hand to tick off, one at a time, the things that the Lord has done.

Additional Word Reasoning

David has just stated that he'll never have to want as a result of his decision in choosing the Lord for his shepherd. As every good student of psychology knows, you'll do a much better job of selling or persuading if you qualify such unilateral conclusions with a couple of whys. It's much like telling a child, "Don't touch that hot stove!" without the explanation: "If you do, you're going to hurt your hand, and you won't be able to use it for a long time." So David does this. Starting with the second verse, he lists the reasons for his choice of the Lord as his shepherd.

Thinking through his words will help us decide where we need our emphasis, pause, and tonal changes.

> He . . . . . . makes me lie down
> in **green** . . . pastures.
> He . . . . . . leads me beside
> **still** . . . waters.

Note first the spacing—the two-second pause—following each "He." This reinforces the fact that God is the subject in the verse, about whom something is being asserted.

Next, wouldn't David want you to pay particular attention to the two adjectives used: "green" pastures—not just any arid pasture—and "still" waters—not unquiet or rushing waters? "Green" and "still" are conditions devoutly to be wished for. These benefits accrue to him only because of his selection of this particular shepherd. A slight emphasis on these two adjectives will make them the focal point of each verse, with a one-second pause after their use for further emphasis.

In verse four, David seems to present even more vigorous reasonings for his selection. Hear his words:

> Even . . . . . . though I walk . . . . . .
> through the valley . . . of the shadow . . .
> of **death** . . . . . .
> I fear **no** evil . . . . . .
> for **thou** art with me.

Doesn't David want us to convey the message quite vigorously about his real feelings that even the face of death strikes no fear in him, because God (this shepherd he has chosen) is with him?

In the next line, I think David wants us to imply in a you-won't-believe-this-but way that even in the presence of his enemies God provides for him:

> Thou preparest . . . a table . . .
> before me . . . . . .
> in the **presence** . . . of my . . . **enemies**.

Here David wants us to understand that he is really saying, "Where in the world are you going to find a shepherd—outside of my Lord—who will take care of you under these circumstances, even in the very presence of your enemies?"

The Wrap-Up

In the first part of the last verse, David wraps up all his arguments, with particular emphasis on the first word, "Surely." He implies that, having told us of his choice, we should understand the power and love of this Lord and realize that only good things will happen to him as long as he lives.

> **Surely** . . . . . . goodness **and** mercy . . .
>   shall follow me
>   **all** . . . the days of my life . . .

The remainder of the verse, and the part David would want us to read more carefully—*and more slowly*—than any other, is:

> and I . . . . . . shall dwell . . . . . .
>   in the **house** . . . .
>   of the **Lord** . . . .
>   **for** ever.

Certainly David would want us to measure each of these words very slowly, very carefully, savoring each one. As we finally, after a *four*-second pause, reach the last words, "for ever," the listener joins David in agreeing that the best choice for a shepherd was indeed made. I cannot emphasize too strongly the absolute need to separate those last words, "for ever," from the preceding ones. This most important step of *emphasis by isolation* was explained in chapter 7, in the section on how to wrap up your sermon. Suffice it to say here that this one word is a sermon in itself; it shows the stability of the nature of the true Shepherd. Not to emphasize this would simply be to read it in robot style.

When the Twenty-third Psalm is used in a funeral service, it will provide the real comfort David wanted to make available only if his words are read in the way David intended: with pride.

Another Psalm, Another Opportunity

Before undertaking a scripture reading, you will need to review every word in every verse. This helps determine which word or words (there's always at least one in every sentence) to emphasize and isolate. When studying them this way, you will recognize which words are most important. Let's look at the first line in Psalm 1.

The first verse of Psalm 1 reads simply, "Blessed is the man who . . ." Right away, one of the words in this verse jumps out and begs for attention. What is the word?

Look again. *Every single word* in that psalm points to the very first word, which is "Blessed," and you should say it with the real emphasis it deserves. The combination of vocal emphasis and a following two-second pause makes this vital word the focal point of the entire verse—and the entire psalm.

You'll remember the importance of this word from having read, in advance of the service, *every word* of this psalm, even though you've read them countless times before. You announce that the Old Testament lesson is Psalm 1. Look up at the congregation with chin raised and with a slight smile on your face (because it is a happy message) and in a clear voice say:

Blessed . . . . . .

You isolate this one word, thereby giving it emphasis. Any word that's not overshadowed by other words stands out by itself. The word "Blessed" should stand out by itself and you should say it *by itself.* And you should wait two full seconds before continuing. Remember, to get a measurement of seconds, simply say slowly, "One second, two seconds, three seconds," etc., and you'll be close to this time interval.

In continuing with the words "is the man who," the words themselves imply that you're going to provide some qualifications for this classification of a blessed man, so you should now separate the word "who." The verse then would read:

Blessed . . . . . . is the man who . . . . . .

Does this sound familiar? It's pretty much the same way that David provided qualifications of why he had selected the Lord for his shepherd. After he said, "I shall not want," he started with "He makes me lie down in green pastures" much as in the First Psalm, where we discover how a blessed person lives and the benefits that accrue as a result of this kind of life. These listings are found in many parts of the Bible.

There is no need to go through the rest of the First Psalm together. Beginning carefully after the word "who," imagine that the writer is ticking off a shopping list by touching each finger (again, mentally) of one hand with the forefinger of the other hand.

Throughout that phase of ministry requiring scripture reading, always review the selection word by word in advance and ask yourself, "David—or Paul, or Lord—how do you want me to read that line today?"

Prefacing Scripture Reading

There is one important procedure, without which the effectiveness of a scripture reading is drastically reduced. This is providing a one- or two-sentence explanation of the context from which the scripture itself comes. I'm always disappointed when a minister says at the point of scripture reading, "Our Old Testament lesson this morning is taken from the book of Exodus, the thirty-second chapter, beginning with the first verse," and then goes directly into the reading of "When the people saw that Moses delayed to come down from the mountain, the people gathered themselves together to Aaron, and said to him, 'Up, make us gods, who shall go before us; as for this Moses, the man who brought us up out of the land of Egypt, we do not know what has become of him.' "

The average lay person who hears these verses in a service feels like saying, "How about that!" Or perhaps, "I wonder how that's going to lead into the sermon?" Or even, "Sounds like one of those strange Bible stories. What's the point?"

Why not share with your congregants a brief picture—if only one short sentence—of the context in which the scripture was written?

In the case of the Old Testament reading just cited, the minister could say, by way of preface, something like this: "We pick up the story of the children of Israel during their Exodus experience at a time when their faith in God is at a low point. They're worried about their present plight and are frightened about prospects for the future. Their leader, Moses, is on the mountain and apparently has been there for some time. The children of Israel are becoming impatient and are worried that he may not return. They turn to Aaron and ask him to make a false idol for them which will go before them and help them continue their journey. Listen to the story of what happens. Listen to the Word of God."

Now, when the minister begins to read the actual words of scripture, the listeners have been brought up-to-date as to the context of the writing. They are then in a far better position to receive the message. They understand the anxiety of the Israelites. And the minister is in a far better position to lay a foundation for that portion of the sermon theme that is based on this passage.

Three quick examples: Duskin ("Dusty") Kenyon, when a student at Union Theological Seminary in Virginia, gave a sermon entitled "Holding Out While Holding On!" She chose, as her Old Testament lesson, Deuteronomy 34. Her preface for reading this chapter was, "This is the story of the death of Moses." How very simple! It was short—not much explanation —but it was enough.

Our minister, Al Winn, whose sermon topic was "Praying for Each Other," selected Genesis 18:16–33 as his Old Testament lesson. Here's what he said: "Our Old Testament lesson outlines the story of Abraham's prayer for Sodom—certainly one of the finest examples of intercessory prayer found in the Bible." This was a little longer than Dusty's explanation, but, again, it set the tone for the scripture reading.

Union Theological Seminary in Virginia student Charles Cornwell, as a student assistant at Second Presbyterian Church in Richmond, gave a sermon entitled "The Ongoing Story." He chose, for his New Testament scripture, Hebrews 11:32 to 12:2. His preface to the reading was brief but magnificent. He simply said, "The account of those who have lived in faith." Again, this gave an indication of the theme that would follow.

We hearers better understand scripture when we get some sort of preface statement. We are drawn into the scripture better when we have some form of introduction to it. We pay closer attention when we have some inkling of what is coming —and we pay closer attention to the sermon because we have a clearer picture of the sermon base which is the scripture. And we may feel we are drawn closer to the minister as a result of the minister's taking that extra bit of time to educate us about the sermon's background.

Repeat Scripture Reference

When referring directly to the scripture itself during the sermon, many preachers make a statement similar to, "As we read in today's scripture lesson, a strong foundational Christian principle becomes readily evident." When this is spoken some ten minutes into the sermon, it is easy to forget the passage being referred to. So, *repeat* the line of scripture. It may be very familiar to the preacher, but can already be forgotten by many people in the congregation.

10

The Importance of Delivery

Many speech experts believe that delivery is largely a matter of personality. Because this quality is so difficult to analyze and even more difficult to alter, potentially excellent speakers may think it's a waste of time to pay attention to delivery. They believe that what and who they are will determine how their speech or sermon comes out. In many cases, they're just thankful for the ability to find something to say. This is negative thinking. As we saw in chapter 9, there is nothing wrong with studying to increase your skills—in preaching or anything else.

How to Direct Your Voice

Much has been written about various manners of speaking. Everyone agrees that speaking from a pulpit is not to be confused with ordinary conversational speaking in terms of volume and enunciation. Don't confuse this statement with what was said in chapter 1 about the need for a conversational tone in preaching. In this chapter, we're talking about the volume of voice and clarity of words within the conversational manner.

To assure proper volume, you should imagine that you're speaking primarily to the last row in the hall. To be successful, you must imagine that your voice is aimed slightly upward at a point about halfway down the sanctuary and about ten to fifteen feet above this point. This lofts the voice above the entire congregation, making certain that it reaches the last pews.

When you consciously project your voice over the congregation in this manner, you automatically create two advantageous conditions: The volume of your voice is somewhat louder because you know you're not simply talking to the first several pews, and your voice is forced into a more measured articulation, because your words can't run together if they're to be grasped by listeners in the back pews.

When you find yourself measuring out and savoring every word to make sure it reaches the back pews, you also find that you are unconsciously adopting a more persuasive delivery. Your intent is for your words to reach the rear of the church; therefore, you measure each carefully.

Let's consider the foregoing delivery suggestions as "enlarged" conversation. In the process, however, you should not consider this enlargement as an oration or a dramatic performance or display. You should utter *each* word to make sure it's not lost in a slurred sentence—so that the congregation can hear it and understand it effortlessly. Speech in this manner is the foundation for the inclusion of gestures and other body movement. These will fit more naturally in an enlarged conversation than in a read or memorized type of sermon.

The Need to Measure Intensity

Hand in hand with the need to project your voice to the last pews, you should also consider the need to vary the intensity of your words. Fortunately, this form of added emphasis, of heightened interest on the preacher's part—the moment when you almost seem to demand more of the listener's interest—comes at about the same spot in every sermon. Mind you, we're not talking entirely about increases in the voice's volume, although that does enter this picture. We're talking about an increase in the intensity of the words—the added emphasis that these words deserve.

The word "intensity" seems to be the best one to describe a concentration of strength in what you are trying to say at that given moment. This word is used in many other homiletic writings, because no one can find a better one. But don't confuse it with the word "emotionalism," which implies a possible lack of control. The word "intensity" means—here—that point where greater emphasis (not necessarily greater volume) is placed on each phrase and, toward the end of the height of the intensity curve, on each word.

Many preachers feel the need to build intensity gradually, all the way from the introduction to the very last minute of the sermon. The listener is then carried to great heights—and left hanging. This is a mistake. It's more important to allow the energy of the sermon to diminish during the closing minutes and to use spaced-out, deliberately spoken, "softer" words to make a lasting impression—more easily taken out of the sanctuary by the listener. (See chapter 7.)

Here is my intensity curve:

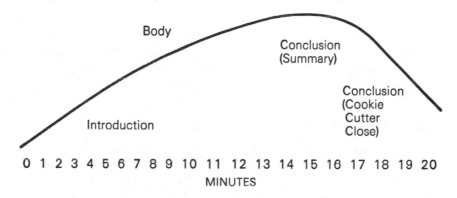

If you're afraid that your voice might be a bit too weak, it may help to build up the intensity of your words as you proceed through the sermon. If you have a weak voice, don't let your voice volume taper off so much out of respect to the drop in the end of this curve to the point that your words are lost and the effectiveness of your message is seriously hampered. Remember that even though your voice intensity may drop in the last few minutes, you are *still* projecting these less intense words to the last pews in the sanctuary.

The Use of Contractions

You'd probably think that, of all the newspapers published, the most formal—the stuffiest—would be *The Wall Street Journal.* Not so. One reason why this paper is so easy to read is that you'll find contractions in practically every sentence, in every article where their use is feasible. This makes for easier reading.

Regardless of how formally written your pulpit notes may be, you can still use contractions in speaking them. Just as contractions make for easier reading, they also make for easier listening. If you're after a conversational, friendly tone in your delivery, use contractions wherever practicable.

There are instances, however, when contractions shouldn't be used, where you are striving for emphasis on certain words. This applies to the sermon conclusion when, as illustrated in chapter 7, proper word and sentence spacing is a must if a concluding thought is to be retained by the congregation. Such is the case in saying, for instance,

"There . . . simply . . . is . . . **not** . . . another method . . . available . . . for salvation."

You certainly wouldn't want to say in a strong, summarizing statement, "There simply isn't another method . . ." because "isn't," as a combination of "is" and "not," cannot be given the heavy emphasis that such a conclusion requires.

A New Word, a New Perspective

We all know many words—what they mean and how they should be used—that seem to stay tucked in our minds until evoked by certain circumstances. This is what happened to one of the words I know but have seldom used, until a Sunday sermon on January 1, 1984.

The date of the sermon is important. It was one of those rare sermons you dream about hearing, with a message so profound—each carefully chosen word had a place of importance —you were shocked and dismayed that it was over before you knew it. The title was "A Time for Every Matter," and it was given by Dr. Patrick D. Miller, Jr., now Professor of Old Testament Theology at Princeton Theological Seminary. He developed in this fine sermon a concept of time as our congregation entered a new year.

But back to the new word. While Dr. Miller didn't actually use it, his masterful presentation evoked it. It was "pacing." His was a deliberate, unhurried delivery containing such thoughts as "Our time is in the hands of God, so look for the gift of time in the new year," and "The time of your being is redeemed by the Lord of time." But—and here's what was so impressive—he seemed to be measuring himself along his points, occasionally pausing with a slight crouch, like a jack-in-the-box ready to spring upward to emphasize his next point, or touching his lips with an upward-pointed finger that suggested a contemplative moment, or leaning forward over the pulpit as if to place added emphasis on a given point. And while there was no hurry about his style, there was also no lag. It was the skill of pacing—deliberately, measuringly, calculatedly crafting words into finished sentences, each of which seemed to settle into its proper place in the whole.

11

The Powerful Pause

This chapter is the only one in the book that has to do with nothing. That's right. It concerns eloquent silence. It's about pauses.

Since these are the places in your sermon when, ideally, nothing happens—you say nothing—you would think this is the easiest part of sermonizing to learn. And in one sense, you can't study it. But you do have to practice it; you really have to practice saying nothing! For this tool—the pause—is a vital, indispensable part of all sermons. It is, in many cases, the *only* tool available to emphasize certain sermon points that would otherwise be joined together so closely that their importance could easily be lost.

No Pause, No Emphasis

Consider this example of how the *lack* of a pause spoiled a wonderful opportunity for emphasis. Here's the statement: "And the gospel answered this poet with a resounding 'no.'" That's exactly the way it was spoken—with a continuous, uninterrupted delivery. Had the preacher said *nothing* for a few seconds, the one word that followed would have carried considerably more importance.

How to say it? How to use the pause? If the preacher nad only said, "And the gospel answered this poet with a resounding . . . . . . *no!*" The dead space—the pause—would have automatically built up a degree of anticipation on the part of the hearers because they had no idea of the concluding part of the statement. This pause, too, provided the natural setting for emphasis on the word "no," which then, by virtue of the pause, became isolated and got the attention it deserved.

Winston Churchill was one of this century's greatest orators. Those of you who have ever heard a recording of his famous speech "We shall fight on the beaches . . ." will remember one of the sentences he spoke so proudly—even defiantly. I'll put dots in his statement where he inserted important pauses.

He said, "If the British Commonwealth and Empire last for a thousand years, men will still say . . . . . . 'This . . . . . . was their finest . . . hour.' " He did not say, "Men will still say this was their finest hour" in the same beat and measure. Read it again and hear the difference.

When you read this famous statement with the pauses inserted, you will hear, "Men will still say . . . . . ."—and there you are hanging, waiting to hear *what* men will still say. Similarly, notice the pause after the word "this." By that time, you have been caught up in the mastery of Churchill's composition, as well as his oratory, as you stand in anticipation of the words that will follow and explain the "this." Even the shorter pause after "finest" creates anticipation. Read it yet again.

Take any sentence at random—inane, insipid, flat—and sprinkle several pauses between natural phrases and see what happens. Reread chapter 7 on how to conclude a sermon, and you'll see how those pauses give meaning and substance to words otherwise lost in a long train of units without character.

One Sunday I complimented Dr. Albert Winn on one of his pauses near the end of his sermon—and this man is a master of the pause! He apparently recognized in me a kindred soul who understood the importance of this tool in preaching, so he told me a story. While amusing, it was serious in pointing out what a pause can do.

A Vermont state legislator, also a Methodist minister, was presenting, without notes, a bill concerning rural education in his state. Halfway through his presentation, his mind went blank. He tried and tried to recall where to pick up on his speech, but he simply couldn't remember. He stood awkwardly before his colleagues until, finally and fortunately, his message started to come back to him. Needless to say, he died a thousand deaths during this period, waiting for his memory to function again, and when he finally finished, he was sure his bill was doomed to failure. But it didn't fail. It passed with a large majority.

After the session, a fellow legislator approached and said, "I've been in this legislature for years, but I have never heard such sincerity and eloquence as you used today. And Bill," he continued, "that pause! I didn't know you could do it. That pause was so dramatic it won over everybody!"

Potentially powerful points are rendered ineffective when they are lost in a string of words and sentences. These points could be spotlighted with the use of a pause. One of your greatest enemies in making strong sermon points is speed of delivery, while one of your greatest assets is the pause.

If you have some trouble getting into this technique, you might start by repeating words that normally precede a key word or phrase. This will automatically provide a pause and, at the same time, lend emphasis to the key word or phrase.

For instance, suppose you wanted to make this statement in a sermon: "What do we mean by the grace of God? Is it not a gift that gives new meaning to the whole concept of life?"

Now, let's make that statement again, but this time we'll repeat certain lead-in words that will force us into pauses. Here it is in its new form: "Is it not a gift . . . a gift that gives a . . . a new meaning to the . . . the whole concept of life?"

This repetition of words creates the impression that you are groping for the proper word, which adds to the freshness that comes out of what seems to be an extemporaneous presentation. Can't you almost see the preacher gesturing with one hand, as if such a motion will help in recalling the proper word or words—and the thought—to be conveyed? The use of a pause makes gesturing easier, too (see chapter 13).

Timing the Sermon for Pauses

Every twenty-minute sermon should include two full minutes of dead air—pauses. One way to prove this theory is to force yourself to compose an uninterrupted eighteen-minute message and then go back through it and drop in pauses at points that need emphasis—particularly in the conclusion. I think you'll agree that 10 percent of the time normally allotted for a sermon is not too much for emphasizing the key points you're trying to make. This is particularly true when you try to avoid the one-paragraph sermon (see chapter 5).

Preaching at too rapid a rate can make a sermon harder to understand. Preachers can get so wrapped up in their message that they want to get it all out as soon as possible. This problem arises either when the sermon is too long, and the preacher has to squeeze it in the normal time period, or when the preacher has some problem relaxing and feeling comfortable in delivering it.

Here the pause will help, even though, in the first case, a too-long sermon is obviously made longer if pauses are used. However, even though it's longer, it will certainly be more interesting. In the second case, where relaxation is a problem, each pause provides a momentary point to get your breath. Did you know that it's less fatiguing to walk slowly than to stand in one spot? The reason is that every time you raise a foot in walking, it has a fleeting moment to relax, which does not happen in a standing position. Similarly, these pauses provide refueling stops along the sermon way.

If you're reluctant to try pausing because you think it's too obvious to the listener, just remember that a pause will seem much longer to you than it does the congregation. You may know in advance how long you're going to make the pause, but they certainly don't.

Remember, too, that a pause is a way to achieve oral punctuation. If you learn to pause, and to do it long enough to build up anticipation on the part of your listeners so that your next point is anxiously awaited, you have developed a kind of poise in their eyes you would not otherwise have. In contrast, a mechanical, rapid-fire delivery may present you as lacking poise—which is to say, lacking confidence and intimacy with your subject.

12

The Influence
of Enthusiasm

Everything said so far concerning the vocal aspects of delivery could well be for naught without the added element of enthusiasm. You know that Charles Dickens had, and probably always will have, a large following because of the stories he wrote. You may not know that while he was alive he had a large following because of the artful way he read these stories to his audiences. He would stand behind the lectern and assume all the characters he had conceived and imitate them all as if he knew them intimately. In the process, he put life and animation into his speaking. He always made enthusiastic presentations and, as a result, always had enthusiastic followers.

Close your eyes and imagine Charles Dickens speaking the words of his characters without this high degree of enthusiasm for which he was famous. Suppose his presentation was dull, lackluster, lifeless, somber, flat, or cold. Do you really think his audiences would have been so large?

Enthusiasm may mean different things to different people. Many of us are turned off by what appears to be the uncontrollable and overly emotional messages of some TV evangelists. This is *not* the kind of enthusiasm I recommend.

How do you get this quality? Why is enthusiasm so important? It's vital because it lights up the preacher, it lights up the pulpit, and it lights up the sermons. The enthusiastic presentation of any subject carries with it a sense of conviction and indicates a sincerity behind the words and a sense of pride in speaking them. This quality also awakens the congregation and makes them alert and receptive to your words.

There's a fellow in our church who is a high-ranking state official. Purely by chance, it seems, he makes some sort of announcement or other at our worship services about once a year. After he's been presented by the minister, he bounces up the pulpit steps, faces the congregation, and smiles. From the moment his mouth opens, only words of enthusiasm come out. No matter the announcement, he has everybody in the palm of his hand. His last presentation started something like this: "What I want to tell you folks this morning is that we've got ahead of us a *beautiful"*—and when he said that word, it really sounded beautiful—"opportunity for all of us to roll up our sleeves and pitch in like a team and do something really big for this church. I'm going to take no more than two minutes to tell you about it now, and I hope you'll be listening very carefully, because all of you can help."

In chapter 3 the point was made that often the best show is not up front but down in the audience. In the case of this fellow's announcement, the faces of those in the congregation always lighted up when they listened to him. All smiles—all smiles.

Let me put it another way. As I write this, we are looking for an executive secretary for our office. We set forth nine clear qualifications for this person and suggested that the personnel agency not send us anyone not totally filling this bill. Then I interviewed two nice women. We rejected them both. The manager of the agency was understandably upset. She said, "Mr. Buerlein, that last applicant had everything you told me you wanted: typing skills, good appearance, experience, education, spelling and proofreading skills—everything you wanted. I can't understand your decision."

I agreed that all the qualifications were there except one: enthusiasm. The agency manager remonstrated that her applicant possessed this quality too and pressed me for details. I groped around for the proper words and finally, in desperation, blurted out, "She simply was not *alive!"*

Many preachers unwittingly set the tone for the entire worship service as soon as they enter the pulpit on Sunday. Watch them carefully, and listen especially closely to their first words. If these words aren't warm and friendly, and if they are not spoken with an *enthusiastic* firmness, both the minister and the words fail at the start to win the concentrated attention they deserve. An alive, alert, and enthusiastic minister can immediately set the tone for a spirited worship service that will be more meaningful, more pleasant, and more rewarding for the congregation. Carry this opening note of enthusiasm through the entire service, right up through the benediction, and the congregation will indeed leave the sanctuary enriched.

A good preacher friend of mine, knowing I was writing this book, discussed this quality of enthusiasm. "My problem is that I, like many preachers, have too much polish and not enough fire. I'm torn," he continued, "between the desire to preach just because I want to say something and the desire to preach because I feel I have something to say. I know the latter feeling is the only true one for a preacher, and I find that the 'something to say' can be more enjoyably and forcefully said if I just create some enthusiasm about it."

He left me with this advice. "Tell those who read your book to review Colossians 3:23 and Hebrews 1:7 (TEV): 'Whatever you do, work at it with all your heart, as though you were working for the Lord and not for men,' and 'God makes his angels winds, and his servants flames of fire.'"

13

Emphasis Through Gestures and Movement

We've all watched people in conversation. How many times have you witnessed this natural act without seeing the speaker make some sort of gesture or movement, however weak?

I remember as a boy trying to get my friends to describe a circular staircase without using their hands. Try it; it's pretty tough. Sign language was used before speech was developed. Because it's fundamental and instinctive, such language accompanies words to a far greater degree than we ever imagine. We often read people more accurately through their actions than through their words. When the two conflict, we tend to trust the actions.

Emphasis Through Gestures

Gestures are really an outward manifestation of inner feelings. The less ardent a person is about a subject, the less the body-mind combination feels disposed to waste a gesture on it. Conversely, the more excited, the more enthusiastic a person is about a subject, the more difficult it is to restrain from gesturing.

Can you imagine yourself caught up in a moving sermon about the way that God's existence and love are seen around the *entire* world without reaching your hands upward, palms up, at least as high as your shoulders, to fortify this description? This is not a theatrical reaction; it's a *natural* reaction.

But exactly when and where to use gestures? They should be used as body or hand movements when needed to augment and emphasize your words. There is such a thing as overdoing it. A constant flurry of arm waving and shoulder shrugging can overshadow content. Particularly to be avoided is wagging one's forefinger at the congregation as if you were scolding them.

One other thing about gestures: Don't use them during scripture reading. Gestures assist you in actually getting the words out of your body and out before the congregation. But these are *your* words, and you are entitled to emphasize them with gestures when appropriate. The reading of the scripture, however, is no time for anything resembling theatrics, nor does Holy Writ need the assistance of gesturing. The input of feeling is enough (see chapter 9).

How should you go about sensing the need for gestures? Get off somewhere by yourself and simply give way to the impulses and sincere convictions you feel about the points in your sermon. Loosen up and relax as you begin to speak these words. Study carefully a particularly strong point you plan to make, digest it, and then exaggerate it in the speaking of it. You've got to learn to let yourself go slightly in using this approach. You might even have to tear the air a little with your hands as long as it helps you make your point.

As you move through this experience, you'll find yourself gesturing, if only to help get these points across with conviction. What you've been doing is the same thing as the baseball player who, striding up to home plate, carries two or more bats with him until he reaches the plate. When it comes time to swing at the ball, his reflexes are stronger, once he is unburdened from the extra bats, and his swing at the ball is more natural and lively.

Practicing gestures is much like carrying an extra bat. You don't plan to go into the pulpit with that extra weight, because excessive gesturing would not be appropriate for the pulpit. However, you'll find yourself in condition to "swing your bat" —to gesture—more naturally.

Finally, you might ask yourself this question: "What are my words saying?" You—and the congregation—may have a better understanding of these words if you help them, and one way to do this is through the restrained use of gestures.

Emphasis Through Pulpit Movement

One of my hopes when visiting a strange church is to find a preacher with enthusiasm and energy—one who is alive. I also hope to see that preacher alive in the sense of not being cemented to one spot, not a "stick in the pulpit."

One of the advantages to listening to a sermon on the radio is that if the preacher suffers from immobility, you can't see it. But if you're there in person and see the minister as if hewn out of the same material as the pulpit, such rigidity can affect your reception of the sermon.

Look at it another way: any movement of a preacher's body during a sermon has to be inspired from within. Such movement, by a one-step turn in either direction, indicates familiarity with the sermon material and a comfort that allows some latitude. Spontaneity of movement in this situation indicates a desire to get closer to one's listeners by carrying on a more intimate conversation with them.

People say that neither gestures nor body movement can be planned. The former may be true, but surely not the latter. I've seen the pulpit notes of any number of preachers, some of which are so marked over as to make neat by comparison the first rough draft of a college term paper.

Prearranged movement cues are quite simple: an arrow pointing either to the right, the left, or back away from the pulpit. These are usually the only three directions in which a minister can move (it would be rare to actually move in front of the pulpit, although I've seen a couple of pulpit arrangements where this is possible).

When should you move? The logical time is between your main points. Remember in chapter 5 we talked about the use of transitional phrases as the natural step between main sermon points. The transitional phrase helps you and the listener shift mental gears, in the same way that the seventh-inning stretch in baseball gives everybody a momentary physical break. A one-step movement to the left or right or backward as the transitional phrase is spoken—or as the next sermon point is approached, with or without such a phrase—similarly provides an opportunity to shift mental gears.

While it may take some practice to use this movement with transitional phrases, there are at least two other times during the sermon when movement is possible and pleasurable. These times occur when you reach those places in your sermon that are so obvious and familiar that a departure from your notes is no problem.

For example, if you're making a doctrinal point that you knew even before you entered the seminary, you can take one step to the right or left of the pulpit and enjoy the relaxation of escaping from your notes, if only for ten to fifteen seconds.

You may be using in your sermon the phrase, "We all believe, of course, in the Trinity of the Supreme Being—Father, Son, and Holy Spirit." That took me twelve seconds to say, which is just enough time for me to walk comfortably to either side of the pulpit, make the statement, and return to the center position and my notes.

Singular Signposts

Pulpit Notes		*Spoken Statements*
Alert—tangible signs	CENTER OF PULPIT	So you see that if you remain alert, you will notice certain tangible signs that show progress is being made in your growth as a Christian.

On the other hand . . .
  Watch imperceptible signs

Don't overlook . . .

Signs indicating faith
  strengthening

Don't forget these will
  also be . . .

Signs indicating love growing

  Conclusion (start)

  Conclusion (finish)

Look at the pulpit notes for the sermon Singular Signposts, which use this arrow-cue method. We'll discuss each movement in turn.

The first comes after the concluding sentence of the first sermon point (which has been spelled out for you). The arrow cues you into taking one short step to the right, letting the left foot join the right foot. Stepping to the right indicates several things. First, you demonstrate visually that you are shifting gears to go from your first point into the beginning of your second. It is almost like saying to the congregation, Come along with me now as we continue to explore other possibilities of this same subject. We left the first point; we are now moving into the second.

After completing the first several sentences of your second point, "Watch imperceptible signs," you may now step back with your left foot (to be joined by your right foot) to your original head-on stance facing the congregation squarely. (This position is indicated by the phrase CENTER OF PULPIT in the middle section.) Your cue for this is the arrow drawn pointing to the left.

Continuing, you may now similarly take a step to the left while stating your introductory transitional phrase, which begins "Don't overlook . . ." and leads into your next point, "Signs indicating faith strengthening." Note the arrow pointing to the left.

After several sentences regarding this point, return to center position as you simultaneously say your introductory transitional phrase, "Don't forget these will also be . . . ," which takes you into your next point, "Signs indicating love growing."

As you move into your conclusion you may wish to step backward one step (draw the arrow pointing to the bottom of your page) and use this position for emphasis. During the last several important sentences of your conclusion (the Cookie Cutter Close), you should step forward into the original normal starting position.

If pulpit movement is carried too far, a literal interpreter might begin to pace back and forth like a caged lion. But there is one more possibility in this area that will make you comfortable and will tend to be reassuring to the congregation. Nor does this movement take you away from your notes. It involves placing your hands on either side of the pulpit—lightly, not hanging on for dear life—and leaning forward ever so slightly at points of emphasis. This can be considered simply a body gesture. You can do it as you look directly ahead or to either side.

If the idea of pulpit movement bothers you, remember that we all had to learn how to walk if we were to move about easily. To be an effective and interesting preacher, you must learn to walk and to move easily about the pulpit, though on a restrained and limited basis. While you don't want to resemble a caged lion, you do want to indicate that you're alert and enthusiastic about the sermon. You're alive—not a stick in the pulpit.

14

Connecting
with Eye Contact

Have you ever been in a small gathering, a meeting, a social function, or a class when the person who was talking never looked directly at you? Did you feel left out? Conversely, have you ever been in a group when the person talking directed his or her words at you? Didn't you feel as though you belonged?

A preacher will find it difficult to look at every single person in the congregation during the sermon in order to make everybody feel that they belong—or at least that some of the words are intended for them. Nevertheless, a good preacher should pay sufficient attention to most of the pew areas within the congregation so that no one feels left out.

Making eye contact with the listening group not only allows the listener to feel included in the sermon remarks, but also provides valuable feedback for you, the preacher, in that you can see listener reaction and change pace if necessary.

The physical arrangement of the building plays an important part in the preacher's ability to maintain eye contact. If the church is in the form of one long room with no balconies, or at least with the balcony at the rear of the sanctuary, the problem is minimized. If, however, the church is like mine, with wings (transepts) at the front and balconies on both sides (even above the wings), the preacher has a real job.

Let's assume that we're talking about a sanctuary with a balcony in the rear and that the average Sunday attendance is 350. While it is virtually impossible for the preacher to look every person in the eye, it is possible to look at these people in groups. Turn your head to the left and let your glance fall on the first five or six pews on that side, and then move slowly on that side toward the rear of the sanctuary in groups or units of five or six pews each. Never mind that you are not looking each person directly in the eye, you are at least looking in their general area, thus creating the impression of almost individual attention. This same type of marching down the rows of pews must be done, obviously, on the right side too. If there's a center aisle as well, use the same procedure. Treat the balcony as one or more separate units, depending upon its size.

But a challenge is really set up in a church like mine where you have endless balconies—even in the wings. Here you would have a couple of avenues open: You can glance downstairs into the left wing and then up above it to the left balcony, then back downstairs to the section of pews on the left of the church, then upstairs to the left balcony above it—and so on. Or (and this is my suggestion), you can keep this eye contact moving on the same floor, starting from the left and moving all the way around to the right, then starting on the upper left balcony and working your way clockwise around the second floor.

One reminder for those of you who wear glasses. If you do *not* let your gaze float around the sanctuary, people seated in certain areas will catch a steady reflection off your eyeglasses. They will not be able to see your eyes or where you are looking. It's a bit disquieting.

If you have ever taken a flash picture of someone wearing eyeglasses, you may have had a blur where the eyes were supposed to be. So remember that if you do wear glasses, it's even more important to move your head about so that parishioners in certain pews don't get this blur for a full twenty minutes. So never just look straight ahead to the neglect of those folks on either side, downstairs, or upstairs—eyeglasses or no eyeglasses.

Perhaps this comment will be said about you: "Every time I listen to the sermon, I feel like my preacher is talking straight to me. It's as if there's nobody else in the sanctuary." Or, as one member said to the other, "The preacher seems to be looking at me, and it makes me uncomfortable." The other member said, "Oh, that's strange, I thought the preacher was looking at me." It's virtually impossible for the minister to continually look at everyone present. But it will *seem* that way to congregants if this procedure of moving your glance about is mastered.

15

How to Handle
Pulpit Tension

At some point or another, the preacher—and particularly the theological student—is faced with the agony often referred to as stage fright. This phrase is poor for several reasons, not the least of which is its association of the preaching of the gospel with a dramatic performance. But the feeling exists. Tensions can be so magnified before a sermon delivery—particularly if there are uncertainties about the sermon—that the effectiveness of the preacher can be reduced. For this reason, the subject should be faced squarely.

More than one board chairman has been rendered an incoherent, quivering mass when addressing a group of peers. Preachers seem to have two good things going for them that work against such tension buildups. The first is that theirs is a noble, sacred cause outside the scope of the average business activity. Second, unlike the business leader, whose listeners are many times equally well—and sometimes better—informed on matters of industry and commerce, the preacher is usually better versed in theology than the congregation. These facts should have the effect of lessening tension on the part of the preacher.

But, if it's seriously interfering with effective sermonizing, let's confront the problem squarely and see what can be done. Here are two little tricks that have always worked for me and may work well for you.

The first trick is borrowed from the famous baritone Lawrence Tibbett. Before every performance, it is said, he would walk up to a corner of a room, face the corner, and call out loudly, "Blah!" I tried it. My cheeks sagged slightly after this word, and it suddenly dawned on me that Tibbett was relaxing his facial muscles. This led to a variation, a silent exercise that is more civil. Squeeze your face with one hand, thumb on one side, fingers on the other. While depressing the cheeks, rotate your hand slowly and, in the process, massage the cheeks. After doing this for a few seconds, remove your fingers and puff up your cheeks, holding them full for no more than two seconds, and then let the air escape slowly. After this, wag your head back and forth slightly in an effort to make cheeks and jowls wiggle a little.

The other trick is borrowed from professional football place-kickers. These specialists, as you know, are reserved for the extra-point situation and generally not used at any other time during the game. Watch them carefully. Several moments before the ball is snapped, of course, they will take a practice kick or two. But they will also let both hands dangle loosely by their sides and jiggle them back and forth as if to shake the tension down their arms and out of their fingertips. You can use this relaxer just before entering the sanctuary for the worship service, for instance.

These are good tension breakers: concentrate on letting your facial muscles sag (by massaging and puffing up your cheeks), and dangle your hands loosely at your sides and shake the tension out of your body through your fingertips.

If the effect of these relaxers is lost after a period of time, there are two additional things you can do in the pulpit. While sitting, you can press your fingertips together, alternating this with tapping them on each other and flexing them back and forth. Or you can force a yawn—well concealed, of course, with a hand. (Better be careful with this one if you're in full view!)

A TV program once presented several days in the life of the British opera star Janet Baker. Not the least profound of her statements about the skills required for her profession was her frank discussion about the buildup of tension.

She described how she had learned to develop a position of expectant joy before a performance. She could not wait to see the fruits of her hours of study, she said. "I feel peaceful and glad that the moment has arrived. I hope to make it the glorious occasion I've worked for."

Her observations are exactly the opposite of "fright," even though her expectations obviously include tension. But hers is a joyful kind of tension that she has learned to develop. It's like waiting at the airport for the return of a loved one. You feel tense waiting for the plane, especially if it's overdue, because you're so anxious to have the person back home. But it's a joyful type of expectation and makes the very act of greeting more meaningful.

Even the greatest speakers and preachers are said to feel some tension before their appearance. Remember the sanctity of your calling and approach your sermon with joyful expectation.

16

How to Develop
the Skill of Practicing

You've heard about the harried New Yorker who comman-
deered a taxi one evening, jumped in the rear seat, and blurted
out, "Quick, how do I get to Carnegie Hall?" The cabbie turned
around and said slowly, "Practice . . . practice . . . practice."

In this same vein, in a 1982 television interview, famous
dancer Fred Astaire was told, "When you dance, Mr. Astaire,
it always looks so natural." Astaire replied, "I'm glad to hear
you say that, but it takes practice—until the dance becomes a
part of you. It certainly takes practice."

Why practice in the first place? After all, you've spent
enough time putting the sermon together to become
thoroughly familiar with the material. Then, too, you have
other pastoral duties demanding your time. You must practice
the sermon in order to be able to think the *thoughts* of the
words and to be able to put them into words *while speaking*,
so that your mental and speaking processes can become coor-
dinated. If you don't do this, the sermon you actually deliver
may be a *different* sermon from the one you prepared and
wrote down. (The wit may say that may not be a bad idea, but
you don't really want that to happen.) Also, remember that
your voice, your gestures, your movement, your enthusiasm
for the subject—all are brought together in the practice session.

A highly beneficial aspect of practicing is that you simulate
the method of communication you will actually use in the
sermon itself. There is a difference in the thought process
when you "speak-practice" aloud and when you "think-prac-
tice" to yourself.

There is real danger in attempting to deliver a sermon you
haven't thoroughly practiced. In chapter 1, I mentioned taping

myself while reading aloud the transcript of a sermon given in a church I visited. The taped sermon didn't sound like either the preacher I had heard or the unspoken tone of the words as they lay on the paper. If you try to deliver a sermon you haven't practiced thoroughly, you will almost be trying to translate the words of another person, because your mental and speaking processes are two different things that have to be tied together. This translation process will be occurring in the pulpit, where you can ill afford the time. You don't want to say to yourself, "Did I write this?"

Three Valuable Tools

Let me suggest three valuable tools for intensive practicing:

1. Finished Pulpit Notes

It does no good to practice sketchy thoughts and amorphous points. You need to hone the sermon to the point where you have final notes. I've strongly recommended the extemporaneous method of preaching which involves sketchy notes (two to four words per line only), or more elaborate notes— almost complete lines but with enough words to provide a safety net if you're not quite up to the full extemporaneous style. I've not included the full manuscript system I hope you ultimately shy away from. But if this is your wish at the moment, then this form of final sermon notes is also what I have in mind for practicing.

In whatever form you wish your notes to be, they should be in a complete, finished state. In other words, if these are to be your guides in the pulpit, there is no need to practice with any other form of cues. Practicing a sermon with unfinished notes is a waste of time and, more importantly, will confuse the actual pulpit presentation.

2. Lectern

There may be some benefit in practicing your sermon under physical conditions different from the pulpit, such as driving your car, mowing the lawn, or eating. Repetition does breed absorption. But while rehearsing under such conditions may be beneficial, you should practice your sermon at least three times under conditions resembling those you find in the pulpit.

Quite obviously, the best place to practice is in the pulpit itself sometime during the week. Assuming that your week's schedule is going as planned, you've probably finished your sermon by Wednesday morning. If such is the case, you may want to practice in the pulpit at least once Wednesday afternoon, once sometime on Thursday, and again, ideally, on Saturday.

Given the total inconvenience in some situations of using the church pulpit itself, I strongly recommend that you try to get a stand-up lectern for your home. This doesn't have to be an expensive, fancy version, just a 12-by-14-inch piece of plywood nailed on a 4-by-4 about 42 inches tall, mounted on a 2-inch piece of wood about 14 inches square. It may be something you or a volunteer congregation member could hammer out. If worse comes to worst, you can always place a cardboard box on top of a card table to simulate a lectern.

But the point is, you need something on which you can place your finished notes, something on which you can place your hand as you practice your one-step movement to the right side, for instance, and something that you can lean on (literally and figuratively) so that your finished notes and the physical pulpit combine to provide a realistic replica of actual pulpit conditions.

3. Quiet

Find a quiet place, free from distracting sounds and noises, for these practice sessions. (The pulpit itself is ideal.) You must have these practice moments in quiet so that you can repeat again and again those phrases which seem to come out awkwardly and which you have to polish. You also need to be able to select the proper places to insert those important pauses.

The poet refers to the quietness of the soul. It is in these quiet practice sessions that you find the calmness needed to firm up a proud sermon.

17

How to Use Humor

The use of humor in a sermon has to be handled most carefully. The pulpit is the last place in the world for a comedian. Too much humor can prove detrimental to a Christian worship service, and poor attempts at humor by the inexperienced can be a disaster. However, the occasional use of humor should endear you to your congregation; they will feel that you are a warm, real human being. They may not remember the actual joke you tell, but they will remember the spirit it added to the sermon, and they will remember *you*—pleasantly.

The Attention-Getting Story

The next time you hear humor in a sermon, look around quickly at the faces of the congregation. You'll notice that suddenly they seem more attentive; they have been jolted from the experience of listening to what might otherwise be an average sermon delivered by an average preacher. If you really want to get your listeners' attention, weave some dignified humor into the situation up front. The outstanding Scottish minister Dr. Murdo MacDonald said at a recent Bible conference that humor and faith are indissolubly related and that humor is a divine gift which God has given us to deal with the immediate problems of human existence. He pointed out that humor, when used sparingly, is a sword of the spirit, but doom awaits the preacher who overdoes it.

Avoid like the plague the use of humor for humor's sake. A good story is fine, provided there is some relevance between it and that portion of the service or the sermon with which it is supposedly connected.

I once attended a seminary class when the students were

giving their first practice sermon. One chap did especially well in his message, which included, as one of his main characters, a tax collector in the New Testament. In a wonderfully warm and friendly manner, this student paused in his sermon and said, "This fellow was a real tax collector; apparently he tried to tax everything he could get his hands on." This light reference created the warm and friendly spirit you should be looking for. It brought to mind a story the student might have used. It goes like this:

> This tax collector reminds me of the state legislator who was making an impassioned plea before his fellow members, trying to get them to remember a previous disaster which might be repeated if they didn't vote for his bill. He called out with upturned hands, "Fellow legislators, let me tax your memory." One member of the budget committee poked the legislator sitting next to him and exclaimed, "Why didn't we think of that?"

Another student in this practice session was making the valid point that God's blessings come to us in various and diverse forms. In this connection, I would have been tempted to tell the story about the tent evangelist who called upon various attendees to stand up and testify as to the blessings they had received. All stood up except one man, who was bent over and needed a cane for support. He was in pretty sorry physical condition. The evangelist spotted him in one of the back rows and called, "Brother, won't you stand up and tell us what the Lord has done for you?" The stooped man rose painfully, leaning on his crutch, and whimpered, "All I can say is, he mighty near ruint me!"

While you should certainly avoid being a stand-up comic, don't rule out the use of a humorous story if it is appropriate to your sermon and, as always, in keeping with the dignity of the pulpit.

Recognizing and Recording

Using the suggestion in chapter 2 about keeping a file on possible sources for sermon materials, don't overlook the many means at your disposal for finding and preserving humorous stories that seem to have spiritual application.

Through the years, I've recorded in brief form such stories with sermonic application. Some of the tabs in this file are labeled Automation, Banks, Baptists, Baseball, Bible, Books, Catholics, Children, Christmas, Church, College—and so on through the entire alphabet. It would be difficult not to find an appropriate story for a talk on any given subject.

This collection of stories has not come easily. I've made notes on scrap paper when I heard a story. I've clipped stories out of church publications and family magazines and saved all sorts of leaflets. Many years ago I used to cut them out of bulletins placed on buses. The only magazine to avoid as such a source is the *Reader's Digest.* This is so heavily read that any story you try to use would probably have already been heard.

This chapter should not be titled "Homer Buerlein's Handy Reference for Funny Church Stories." However, here are just a few of hundreds of stories, chosen to point out the possible uses of anecdote as a sermon tool. In each case, the introductory words are those of the minister.

Collecting Usable Stories

Christmas pageant. "I want to remind the congregation of our annual Christmas pageant to be held in the dining hall next Thursday night. Much work has gone into this, especially by our younger people.

"I heard about one six-year-old boy who rushed home to tell his mother he'd been given a role in the pageant. His mother naturally asked what part he had been given. The boy replied excitedly, 'I'm a wise guy.' "

College break. "I'd like to welcome home for the spring break the many college students I see in our congregation this morning. It's a pleasure to have you all back, and I know you're enjoying this brief rest. Incidentally, I heard about one student who sent the following telegram to her father: 'I'm worried about you. Haven't heard from you in weeks. Please send a check immediately so I'll know you are OK.' "

Bible study. "From time to time we talk about the need to keep our faith strong through frequent Bible reading. I know it is sometimes difficult for the untrained lay person to get through some of the esoterica of Holy Writ, but there are adjunct studies available, not to mention the help you can get from our Sunday school and other courses.

"So you won't feel you're alone if sometimes you have trouble following the scripture, let me remind you of a conversation between a Sunday school teacher and her adult class.

"She asked, 'How far, in miles, is Dan from Beersheba?'

"One of the students asked, 'Do I understand these are the names of places?'

" 'They are indeed,' replied the teacher.

" 'That's a new one on me,' the student admitted. 'I always thought they were husband and wife, like Sodom and Gomorrah.' "

Shortening the sermon because of other activities. "You all know that we will have our important business session immediately following worship, so I'll let you know in advance that I have a shorter sermon this morning.

"I feel somewhat like the teacher who asked the student why his composition on milk was only one-half page long when he was asked for two full pages. The student replied, 'I wrote about condensed milk.' "

The need to practice Christian principles. "Most of us know what we should be doing in connection with setting our faith into motion and lending our visible active support to our church. But we all slip occasionally, as shown by this story.

"Two men were out fishing one Sunday morning when they heard church bells ringing in the distance. 'You know, Bill, we really ought to be in church,' one of them said.

" 'Well,' the other one answered, 'I couldn't go anyway. My wife is sick.' "

Acknowledging the work of a church school staff and encouraging attendance. "We all owe a lot to our faithful church school teachers who do such a wonderful job in bringing our youngsters to a knowledge of the Bible and precepts for Christian living.

"I once heard of such a teacher of preteen youngsters who had a course on the Ten Commandments. ' "Honor thy father and thy mother" tells us how we should treat our parents,' she explained on one occasion. 'I wonder if you could quote a commandment that tells us how to treat our brothers and sisters?'

" 'Yes,' replied one ten-year-old child. ' "Thou shalt not kill." ' "

As these few examples indicate, almost any good Christian joke has potential for more than one occasion, not just the one for which it seems primarily intended. For instance, the story about the youngster who is excited about his "wise guy" role in the Christmas pageant could just as well be used in recognizing the faithful labor of the church school workers as they provide varied programs for church youth—not just at Christmas. This same story could also be used instead of the Dan/Beersheba, Sodom/Gomorrah story in connection with the need for diligent Bible study, if only to correctly understand biblical terms (wise guy vs. wise men).

Or take the story about the fisherman who couldn't attend church anyway because his wife was sick. In addition to—or instead of—using it to encourage the need to put Christian principles into action, you could use it to encourage attendance at any church function.

As a last example of story flexibility, take the one about the worried college student who sent the telegram home requesting a check immediately. This can be used interchangeably between those sermons normally preached near Mother's Day and Father's Day to provide an example of the taken-for-granted beneficence of one's earthly father, much as we do in the case of our heavenly Father.

In short, don't be surprised if you can take almost any given story and make it conform to an occasion at hand. Just to be funny without relevancy is a mockery to the pulpit and should be avoided. But you can use a really good anecdote as a step in expanding a larger idea.

I'm a strong believer in the formality of a church worship service and certainly the role of the sermon in it. I have deep respect for the seriousness of the gospel message; it would be difficult to spot humor in the story of everlasting life. But it is essential to have at your disposal something that will penetrate the iciness of cold formality and increase the *receptivity* of your congregation. That something can be humor.

18

Other Parts of the Worship Service

In addition to composing and delivering sermons, there are several areas in the order of worship about which I've been concerned over the years. Even though they're not directly related to the sermon, they will have an indirect effect on the sermon by establishing the atmosphere in which the sermon is received.

Welcome

The worship service needs to begin with the recognition and adoration of the sovereignty of God. This is certainly the foundation upon which every worship service is built.

Some ministers will leave the pulpit seat, stand up, as a signal for the service to begin, and then say something like, "Good morning. I welcome you all to our morning worship service as we gather together in the worship of God." The minister then invites the congregation to stand. The worship gets off to a good start with both a friendly greeting and the expression of proper adoration. Contrast this with the service in which the minister approaches the pulpit and, arms extended, palms upward, motions for everybody to rise, following which the adoration is proclaimed—with no welcome.

It's a small point, perhaps, but the preliminary welcome is like a verbal handshake. It says to the congregation, "We're glad you're here to join us in this worship service, and we want you to know that you're certainly welcome." Formality is important, but the informality of a warm welcome will add to the attractiveness and meaning of the worship service.

Hymns

Many of us love to sing hymns—especially those we know well. There's nothing quite like singing a hymn without the need to read every word because we know most of it by heart.

In some churches the opening hymn is slow and unfamiliar. This makes me feel I'm in strange territory—maybe even right out of my denomination. But to stand up, even in a strange church, and start right off with "A Mighty Fortress Is Our God," "Lead On, O King Eternal," "Immortal, Invisible, God Only Wise," or "Holy, Holy, Holy" makes me feel I belong. My religious and mental feet are on solid ground, ready to accept the rest of the service.

The same thing goes for the closing hymn. There is nothing worse than hearing a congregation stumbling through an unfamiliar hymn just before the benediction. I'm not against unfamiliar hymns; what is unfamiliar to one person may be well known to another. Some unfamiliar hymns may have strong relevancy for the sermon for that Sunday, while some of the more familiar hymns may not be applicable.

But the minister, together with the organist and whatever committee is responsible for the worship service, should know with which hymns the congregation is familiar. If your service normally contains three hymns and one of them is less familiar (and certainly less stirring) than the other two, place it somewhere in the middle of the service, rather than at the opening or closing. These two spots have the greatest need for spirited participation.

Benediction

In most cases, a church service will close with a strong hymn, and while everyone is standing, they will be dismissed with the benediction. This is usually one of the old standbys: "May the Lord bless you and keep you . . ." or "May the grace of our Lord Jesus Christ . . ." These are fine, and I look forward to being dismissed with one of them.

However, it's even better to see as the first sentence of the benediction a one-line summary of the sermon theme. This repetition fortifies the main message of the sermon and lets the congregants leave the sanctuary with both this theme and the benediction figuratively ringing in their ears. Try starting with the phrase "Let us leave this place with the knowledge that . . ." and add one line that summarizes the sermon, followed by the actual benediction itself.

If the sermon had to do with the subject of suffering (in the style of Job), a benediction could be: "Let us leave this place with the knowledge that our heavenly Father, though unseen, is available to us in times of suffering through the gift of prayer; and that his Son, Jesus Christ, who is our Great Physician, can heal our sorrows and wounds through his abundant love and his eternal life. . . . . . And now, may the grace of our Lord Jesus Christ, the love of God . . ."

If the sermon is the last item in the worship service, to be followed by the benediction, no one-line summary is necessary because the sermon with its own summary should still be fresh in the minds of people as they leave the sanctuary. If, however, the sermon is separated from the benediction by a hymn or any other item, the thrust of the sermon cannot afford to be lost and should be carried over into the benediction.

In any event, it's a good idea not to insert announcements, officer-induction exercises, and the like between the sermon and the benediction. The theme of the sermon and the opening sentence of the benediction should be the same and should be fairly close together.

After the Benediction, What?

Sometimes minor bedlam takes place when the service is over and the minister tries to get to the greeting post. Actually, the service is not over until the minister has left the sanctuary and gone to this post.

This disorder usually sets in when the minister offers the "Amen" and becomes caught at the front of the sanctuary. The congregation, usually out of respect for the minister's position, will stand and wait politely for him to go out. To avoid this, why not let the choir sing an "Amen"? While this refrain is being sung, there is plenty of time for the minister to get to any other point in or just outside the sanctuary in an orderly, reverent manner before the congregation has an opportunity to disband.

The finest way to handle these closing seconds—truly the smoothest way conceivable—is for the minister to pronounce the entire benediction while slowly walking down the aisle toward the rear of the church. With just a few practice runs, you can gauge both the speed of your uttering the benediction and your gait down the aisle. This timing can be practiced on one of those Fridays or Saturdays when you have a sermon dry run in the empty sanctuary. The length of the benediction will be about the same, even if it includes the one-line summary suggested above. This practice will determine at what point down the aisle you should begin the total benediction so that it will be completed about the time you reach the last pew.

A service that is opened as if it were planned and closed on a well-organized note indicates your care for the congregation and care for the entire service.

A Prayer

Assuming that prayer is a daily practice with you as it is with me, I do not presume to advise you of its power. I cannot, however, refrain from telling you what a source of power prayer has been to me in engaging in church activities, most of which I feel inadequate and unworthy to perform. I prayed every time I took up my dictaphone in pulling this book together, and I also prayed whenever I was speaking or preaching on church occasions.

Let's close this book with a prayer that you may find to be a source of strength.

Dear Lord, give me the boldness of Paul and make me a person of action in the pulpit this morning. Remove my timidity, but share with me your calmness and your serenity. Give me a good sense of recall and make my words attractive, truthful, and meaningful so that those who hear will be drawn closer to you.

Make me a firm and steady person—a strong kingdom representative—your witness for this place and time. In Jesus' name. Amen.